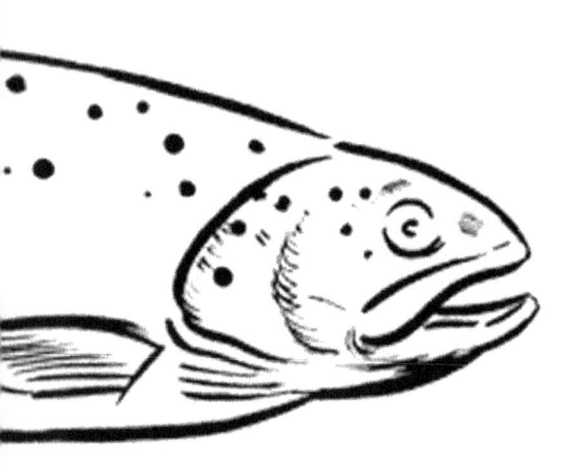

2 Guys and a River

the
FLY FISHER's
BOOK of
LISTS

LIFE IS SHORT. CATCH MORE FISH.

Dave Goetz and Steve Mathewson

The Fly Fisher's Book of Lists: Life is short. Catch more fish.

Copyright © 2017 by David L. Goetz and Steven D. Mathewson. All rights reserved.

Printed in the United States of America.

No part of this book may be used or reproduced in any manner whatsoever without written permission except in the case of brief quotations embodied in critical articles and reviews in print and online media, and social platforms including but not limited to Twitter, Facebook, Instagram, LinkedIn, Pinterest, and Google Plus.

For bulk sales of this product, visit www.2guysandariver.com, or email Dave Goetz or Steve Mathewson at: stevedave@2guysandariver.com.

Illustrations and design by Amanda Duffy (ratunderpaper.com).

Big Snowy Media edition published 2017.

Library of Congress Cataloging-in-Publication Data

Goetz, David LaRue, 1962 -

Mathewson, Steven D., 1961 -

The Fly Fisher's Book of Lists: Life is short. Catch more fish.

1. Fly Fishing - United States 2. Fishing - United States 3. Outdoors - United States

I. Title

ISBN: 978-0-9852655-7-1

Acknowledgments

I dedicate this book to my brother, Matt. I took him fly fishing to Montana when he was 16 and ignored his cries for help when he gashed his leg trying to fish a beaver pond. "Greedy, greedy, greedy," I said as I moved past him and quickly started fishing the next pond. I owe him one.

— Dave

I dedicate this book to my brother, Dave. When we were both in high school, we split the cost to buy a cheap fly rod complete with an even cheaper reel and level line. Thanks to some forgiving brookies, which kept rising to take our dry fly in the center of its nest (made by our leader!), we became hooked on fly fishing for life.

— Steve

Table of Contents

Introduction vi
Bob's 8 Pearls of Fly Fishing Wisdom 2
5 Traits of the Successful Fly Fisher 4
The 3 Biological Drives of Trout 6
6 Common Dry Fly Attractor Patterns 8
11 Reasons You're Not Catching Trout 10
6 Ways to Spoil Your Guided Trip 12
5 Ways to Be a Conservationist 14
10 Commandments of Wading 16
3 Fly Fishing Lessons From My Father 18
Nymph Fishing's 7 Nagging Questions 20
5 Tips for Fly Fishing Lakes 22
5 Reasons I (Steve) Took Up Fly Tying 24
6 Reasons I (Dave) Don't Tie Flies 26
3 Disciplines to Master Spring Creek Fly Fishing 28
8 Additional Safe Wading Tips 30
7 Ways to Make the Most of Public Access 34
5 Quick Tips to Catching More Trout on Hoppers 36
6 Planning Tips for Your Fly Fishing Trip 38
3 Reasons Why I (Steve) Fly Fish 40
10 Reasons to Fish the Yellowstone Ecosystem 42
7 Fly Fishing Safety Devices 44

8 Fly Fishing Personalities 46
4 Ways to Encourage Your Kids to Fly Fish 48
3 Truths about the Mother's Day Caddis Hatch 50
4 Questions before Buying Your First Fly Rod 52
Dave's 5 Favorite Nymph and Wet Fly Patterns 54
Steve's 5 Favorite Nymph and Wet Fly Patterns 56
5 Questions before You Buy Your Next Pair of Waders 58
6 Elements of a Satisfying Day on the River 60
7 More Safe Wading Tips 62
5 Wild Animals to Observe at a Distance 64
5 Precautions to Take While Fly Fishing 66
12 Simple Fly Fishing Hacks 68
4 Practices to Break Out of a Fly Fishing Slump 70
5 Common Fly Fishing Dangers 72
5 Disciplines to Fly Fish More 74
4 Ways to Make Fly Fishing Simple 76
3 Takeaways from "A River Runs Through It" 78
5 Tips When Fishing the Yellowstone Ecosystem 80
4 Reminders Before You Fish a Hatch 84
5 Lessons from a Recent Fly Fishing Trip 86
8 Stupid Things We've Done While Fly Fishing 88
9 Items to Weather the Weather 90

Table of Contents

3 Ways to Track Your Adventures 92
8 Tips to Start "Mousing" 94
Our 6 Favorite Outdoor Authors 96
The 3 Kinds of Rivers You'll Fly Fish 98
8 Adjustments to Make for Spring Creeks 100
Our 6 Favorite Eateries in the Yellowstone Ecosystem 102
5 Questions before You Set Up Your New Reel 104
8 Smart Reactions When You Fall into the River 106
5 Truths When Fishing Dry Flies After Dark 108
7 Spots to Cast Your Dry Fly 110
4 Notes on Fly Fishing Knots 112
3 Half-Truths of Fly Rods 114
3 Humbling Fly Fishing Moments 118
3 Adjustments When Fishing Streamers on Smaller Creeks ... 122
4 Benefits of a Fly Fishing Buddy 126
5 Reasons You Need a Wading Staff 130
7 Tips for Better Fly Fishing Photos 134
10 Ways to Cope with the Fly Fishing Off Season 138
7 Strategies to Fly Fish in Winter Without Losing It 142
5 Problems with Your Cast and How to Fix Them 146
9 Fly Fishing Moments that Require Different Speeds 150
5 Unlikely Places to Catch Trout 154

Interpreting the 4 Feeding Behaviors of Trout	156
7 Basic Facts About Mayflies	158
4 "More" Fly Fishing Myths	160
Tag Index	164
About the Fly Fishers	168
About the "2 Guys and a River" Podcast	170

"THIS BOOK WAS MEANT TO BE CONSUMED LIKE A BAG OF POTATO CHIPS. GRAB A HANDFUL. AND THEN WALK AWAY... IF YOU CAN."

Introduction

10 POINTS TO INTRODUCE OUR BOOK OF LISTS

This was a blast to assemble. The many lists come from our blog, podcast, and half-baked, middle-aged brains.

Some important things to remember:

1. There is no finite number of lists.
There are thousands of lists. You know that. We know that. We compiled a few organized around how our brains (which very likely won't be preserved for future science research) work.

2. There is a half-life to every list.
The lists work now. Or at least some of the points in some of the lists worked at one point. These are practical and fun. Some are tongue-in-cheek. If you disagree with a point, fine. Send us an email (stevedave@2guysandariver.com) and give us a different list or correct us.

3. These are not eternal truths or timeless principles.
This is a corollary to #2. Just needed to say it more clearly and one more time.

4. We keep repeating ourselves.
We didn't run out of material. We just feel the need to keep mentioning bear spray, wading belts, the need to moisten your knot, etc. The repetition is a window into ideas we think are, well, worth repeating.

5. This book is meant to be consumed like a bag of potato chips.
Grab a handful. And then walk away. Leave the rest for another time. If you can.

6. We hope you make a fly fishing trip to Bozeman, Montana.
That's our happy place. Be sure to check out the list with the top eateries in the Yellowstone Ecosystem.

7. Fly fishing is pure joy.
Just had to write that. We'd hate to do it for a living, because then it would be more like work. We would make lousy guides. Then again, we do get joy from teaching others how to fly fish.

8. We'd love your lists.
Yes, we'll probably steal an idea or two. But we'll try to give you credit. Visit our web site at 2guysandariver.com and post your ideas on one of our articles. Or email us at stevedave@2guysandariver.com.

9. Subscribe to our podcast.
That's the heart and soul of it all.

10. Keep fly fishing.
And mentor someone who is just starting out. Enjoy.

Steve   Dave

Inspiration

BOB'S 8 PEARLS OF FLY FISHING WISDOM

Steve's mentor was a retired fireman by the name of Bob Granger, a veteran fly tyer and guide to the stars. He guided folks like President Jimmy Carter and baseball legend Hank Aaron. Steve took a fly tying class from Bob, and they struck up a friendship. Here are eight of Bob's (many) pearls of fly fishing wisdom:

1. Nymph (and streamer) fishing is most productive.
This is for all you dry-fly-only fishers. The cold hard truth is that 85 to 90% of a trout's diet comes from below the river's surface. Use nymphs or streamers to catch more fish.

2. The best weather for fly fishing is an overcast, cool day.
A sunny day is often the worst. To catch the hogs (the big trout), try a streamer on a dark, overcast day or during times of low light in the early morning or late evening.

3. An old extension cord will provide you with a lifetime of copper wire for fly tying.
Too bad other fly tying materials are not as abundant – and cheap!

4. The time to fish mayflies and caddis is different.
To fish during a mayfly hatch, the best time is mid-day, between 11 and two. But if you are fishing during a caddis hatch, the evening is when the majority of caddis flies emerge.

5. Tie your nymph and streamer patterns with beadheads.
While this tends to be standard today, it wasn't "back in the day." Beadheads create a natural drift. If you insist on weighting your flies in another way, use a different color thread for your weighted flies to tell them apart from the non-weighted flies.

6. The more you fly fish, the fewer flies you will use!
For dry fly fishing on the Yellowstone or Gallatin Rivers, a Parachute Adams or an Elk Hair Caddis will work much of the time.

7. Change the size of fly before you try another pattern.
If the fish are picky, you may also want to check your tippet size. Remember, the larger the number, the smaller the tippet size. A 5x tippet tied to a size #20 fly might look like a rope, so go with a 6x.

8. Now mend your line.
Bob is the eternal voice inside Steve's head.

Inspiration

5 TRAITS OF THE SUCCESSFUL FLY FISHER

Fly fishing is a sport for a lifetime. Not every one who picks up a fly rod, though, stays with it. Here are five traits of those who do:

1. Problem Solver
This person assumes that each day on the river will bring new challenges to overcome or problems to solve.

2. Persistent
This fly fisher perseveres through the learning curve of tying new knots, finding new waters, trying new techniques, and enduring slow days on the river.

3. Kinesthetic Learner
This means the fly fisher is okay with learning by failure; he or she learns by doing. What other way to learn is there?

4. Humble
This person doesn't blink at asking the stupid questions.

5. Listener
We steal more great ideas about where to fly fish or what flies to use by overhearing folks yammer on about their great success. Especially in fly shops.

"THE SUCCESSFUL FLY FISHER PERSEVERES THROUGH THE LEARNING CURVE OF TYING NEW KNOTS, FINDING NEW WATERS, TRYING NEW TECHNIQUES, AND ENDURING SLOW DAYS ON THE RIVER."

Education

THE 3 BIOLOGICAL DRIVES OF TROUT

A big tip of the hat to Gary Borger (garyborger.com) for these three biological drives of trout. They are important because they may help you figure out where the fish are located.

1. Self preservation
"Save your butt." An undercut bank, a deep pool, or the current by an obstruction (a rock, a tree branch) provides protection for a trout. These "sheltering lies" are a great place to cast your fly, though often not the easiest to fish.

2. Getting something to eat
"Feel your gut." Look for the bubbles (foam line) in the current. This is the cafeteria where the trout look for food. Don't ignore these "feeding lies" when you're deciding where to cast. Slow down to read the river before you cast.

3. Reproduce
"Make kids." Trout will often lurk downstream from spawning beds (the redds) waiting for eggs. But be a good conservationist and stay off the redds!

> "LOOK FOR THE BUBBLES (FOAM LINE) IN THE CURRENT. THIS IS THE CAFETERIA WHERE THE TROUT LOOK FOR FOOD."

Flies

6 COMMON DRY FLY ATTRACTOR PATTERNS

Sometimes you need the exact dry fly pattern to catch selective trout. But when there is no apparent insect hatch, it's time to pull out an attractor pattern if you insist on dry fly fishing. The strategy is to coax the fish to the surface rather than to match the insects on which they are feeding. It's attraction rather than imitation. When we're not fishing a specific hatch, we like them in sizes #14, #16, and #18. Here are six common patterns:

1. Parachute Adams
It can imitate midges or Blue-Winged Olives or mosquitoes.

2. Elk Hair Caddis
Yes, we're aware that this is technically not an attractor pattern. But this tan fly (which also comes in a black version) simply looks "buggy." It's also easy to see on the water.

> "WHEN THERE IS NO APPARENT INSECT HATCH, IT'S TIME TO PULL OUT AN ATTRACTOR PATTERN IF YOU INSIST ON DRY FLY FISHING."

3. Red or Yellow Humpy
The elk hair hump and the generous brown hackle at the front of the fly make this float forever.

4. Royal Wulff
There is a whole family of "Royal" flies, beginning with the Royal Coachman — America's first great fly pattern, according to Paul Schullery, who wrote an entire book on it!

5. Renegade
An unusual looking fly with white hackle at the front and brown hackle at the rear, some fly fishers fish it as a wet fly (beneath the surface).

6. Spruce Moth
Technically, this fly is also an imitation, but also works as an attractor because it is big (easy to see) and has plenty of hackle (so not easily water-logged).

Tactics

11 REASONS YOU'RE NOT CATCHING TROUT

It has been a long day. You are batting .000. Maybe the fish are simply not biting.

Or maybe you're not catching trout because of one or more of these 11 reasons:

1. It's a bright sunny day.
Often you'll have better luck on overcast days. The exception seems to be when you're fishing hoppers.

2. Your fly is too big.
Make sure you have multiple sizes of the same fly in your fly box. Go smaller.

3. You cast like your mama.
Unless your mama wears wading boots.

4. Your dead drift looks like a rubber ducky with spasms.
Your presentation is almost always the problem. Mend your line to reduce the drag on your fly (and those annoying spasms).

5. You scared 'em.
You should not have walked up to the run like a drunk Abominable Snowman.

6. The run was just fished.
Find a smaller stream with no crowds.

7. It's too early.
If you are gunning for huge browns, then maybe fishing at 4:30 a.m. is a good idea. Otherwise, you may be too early.

8. You haven't moved from the run in 30 minutes.
Fly fishing isn't bass fishing from shore, so keep moving.

9. The river is blown out.
If the river or stream is like chocolate milk, head back to your truck, jump on your phone, and watch a movie on Netflix.

10. You're not deep enough.
Add some split shot to your nymph rig or move your strike indicator up your leader.

11. You have the wrong fly.
Know your hatches and patterns. Buy a book. Take an online class. Find a mentor.

Trips

6 WAYS TO SPOIL YOUR GUIDED TRIP

It's easy to spoil your guided trip, if you are so inclined:

1. Do not communicate your limitations or expectations.
After all, your goal is to impress your guide, so pretend you know more than you really do.

2. Ignore your guide's advice.
You know better than he or she does, right? It's not like you're shelling out big bucks for someone else's expertise and wisdom.

3. Expect the perfect day.
You have, uh, a right to expect that the weather conditions and water conditions will be perfect.

4. Forget about your surroundings since you are on a mission to catch fish!
No worries if you miss the five-point (Western count) buck in the

brush near the bank, or the bald eagles perched on the high branches of a Cottonwood tree. You've paid big money to catch fish, and that's all.

5. Assume your guide will have all the clothing you need.
The weather never changes, and weather forecasts are always spot-on. It's likely that your guide has every article of clothing you need in YOUR size.

> "SINCE YOU ARE THE ONLY BRIGHT ONE IN THE DRIFT BOAT, THERE'S NO NEED TO BE CURIOUS AND YOU SHOULD NEVER ASK QUESTIONS OF THE GUIDE."

6. Never ask a question of your guide.
Since you are the only bright one in the drift boat, there's no need to be curious.

Education

5 WAYS TO BE A CONSERVATIONIST

Whenever you set out for the river with fly rod in hand, don't forget to bring along your conservation hat:

1. Pick up after others (and yourself).
It goes without saying that you should pack out your own trash — wrappers, beverage containers, even old leaders.

2. Land your fish quickly and release it slowly.
After netting a fish as quickly as you can, slow down and gently hold the fish in the water, letting it recover and get its bearings... even if it takes more than a few seconds.

3. Obey every fishing regulation.
Do the simple things like use barb-less hooks, lead-free flies, and non-toxic split shot when the regulations require them.

4. Stay off the redds!
When you fish in the spring when the rainbows and cutthroats are spawning, or in the fall when the browns run, keep off the redds – that is, the spawning beds.

5. Give fish a break during low water and high temps.
This is typically an issue in the "dog days" of late July, August, and early September.

> "AFTER NETTING A FISH AS QUICKLY AS YOU CAN, SLOW DOWN AND GENTLY HOLD THE FISH IN THE WATER, LETTING IT RECOVER AND GET ITS BEARINGS... EVEN IF IT TAKES MORE THAN A FEW SECONDS."

Safety

10 COMMANDMENTS OF WADING

The lawgiver who delivered these was not Moses, but Duane Dunham – a veteran fly fisher and friend who presented these to his fly fishing class at a community college in Oregon.

1. The faster the river is flowing, the lower the depth level you can wade.
This means wading only mid-thigh in swift water.

2. Keep your strides short.
Panic leads to larger strides, which can result in getting stuck in the current with your feet about a yard apart.

3. Make sure you have the right soles.
Though controversial, felt soles tend to give fly fishers better footing, especially in fast-moving rivers with smooth-rock bottoms like the

Yellowstone River. There are a variety of soles for wading boots; know which is best for the rivers you fish.

4. Use a wading staff.
You can purchase one, use an old ski pole, or simply use whatever stout branch you can find along the river's edge.

5. Angle downstream when crossing a river.
This enables you to work with the current, not against it.

6. Don't try to turn around in fast current!
Sidestep or back up carefully.

7. Wear a wading belt with your chest waders.
It keeps your chest waders from filling up with water if you slip and take an unexpected bath. Never wade without one.

8. If you fall in, don't try to stand up too quickly.
Keep your feet down river and stay in a sitting position and wait until you reach knee-deep water before you try to stand up.

9. Let your fly rod go.
Gulp. If you need to use your hands to stroke to shore, give it up. You can replace your fly rod (and get the latest model!), but you can't replace yourself.

10. Don't wade fish alone!
At least avoid certain rivers or stretches or runs if you insist on fishing alone.

"WADE ONLY MID-THIGH IN SWIFT WATER."

Inspiration

3 FLY FISHING LESSONS FROM MY FATHER

These three lessons my (Steve's) dad taught me came during the handful of times he took me trout fishing with a spinning rod or during the dozens of times he took me hunting for pheasants, white-tail deer, or elk:

1. Be patient with youngsters.
There should be a Chinese proverb that says, "Teach a child to fish and try not to go crazy in the process."

2. Invest in quality equipment.
When it came to hunting, my dad did his research and purchased high-quality firearms. The scopes on our rifles didn't fog up when the cold and moisture clashed. Don't skimp if you want to succeed. The place to spend more money in fly fishing equipment is on your fly rod and wading boots.

3. Work together as a team.
When I hunted with my dad, there was usually another brother involved – either one of his or one of mine – and we learned to make our team work to our advantage. During archery season, we often got shots at bull elk because the guy using a call would set up about 10 yards behind the shooter. It works a little differently with fly fishing, of course. But two can be better than one when it comes to problem solving. And it's safer, too.

> "THERE SHOULD BE A CHINESE PROVERB THAT SAYS, 'TEACH A CHILD TO FISH AND TRY NOT TO GO CRAZY IN THE PROCESS.'"

Tactics

NYMPH FISHING'S 7 NAGGING QUESTIONS

Fly fishing with nymphs is one big ongoing challenge. Here are seven questions that nag at fly fishers:

1. Do I have enough weight?
The goal is to get the nymph or wet fly down to where it belongs: rolling along the bottom of the run. Often you need another split shot or two.

2. Is my top fly at the right depth?
Make continual adjustments to your strike indicator when at work on the river.

3. Should I use a dropper or trailer fly?
If you're just starting out, get comfortable fishing with a single fly. Then go with two. Or three (if you're really ambitious and don't mind increasing the risk of a tangled mess).

4. Am I mending well enough?
No, you're not. This is the chronic challenge of fishing nymphs. Keep at it!

5. Is the twitch a strike?
Newbie fly fishers tend to be slow to strike (or "set the hook") when the strike indicator twitches or dips below the surface.

6. Should I change my fly?
This should not be your first move when you're not catching trout, but maybe your second.

7. Which fly should I try next?
Go smaller or try a slightly different color.

> "DO I HAVE ENOUGH WEIGHT? THE GOAL IS TO GET THE NYMPH OR WET FLY DOWN TO WHERE IT BELONGS: ROLLING ALONG THE BOTTOM OF THE RUN"

5 TIPS FOR FLY FISHING LAKES

We call our podcast "2 Guys and a River" for a reason. We love rivers. But we also like to fly fish high mountain lakes. Here are five quick tips:

1. Do your homework.
Many fly fishers don't take the time to learn anything about the lakes they intend to fly fish. Begin by engaging the shop monkey at the local fly shop.

2. Don't ignore the shoreline.
Early morning or early evening is a perfect time to find feeding fish along the shoreline of a lake.

3. Go deep.
When fish are not feeding on the lake's surface, it's time to fish streamers.

4. Try a float tube.
This is a convenient, inexpensive way to make your way around a small lake. Be sure to wear a life preserver!

5. Fish the inlet and outlet if you can.
The trout will sometimes congregate in these places because the food line is rich.

> "FISH THE INLET AND OUTLET IF YOU CAN. THE TROUT WILL SOMETIMES CONGREGATE IN THESE PLACES BECAUSE THE FOOD LINE IS RICH."

Flies

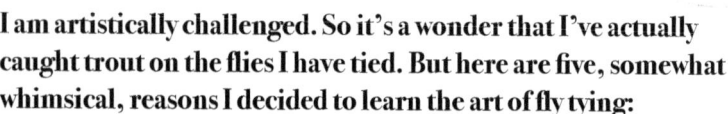

5 REASONS I (STEVE) TOOK UP FLY TYING

I am artistically challenged. So it's a wonder that I've actually caught trout on the flies I have tied. But here are five, somewhat whimsical, reasons I decided to learn the art of fly tying:

1. It would help me learn to say "tying flies" rather than "flying ties."
If you've never made that mistake, then you won't understand. By the way, it didn't help.

2. It would put hoarded stuff to good use.
I could buy a top-of-the-line fly rod if I had a 10-spot for every time a friend said, "Here, I thought you might want this for fly tying material."

3. It would allow me to use the feathers and hides I have collected from hunting trips.
I lived my dream of catching a trout on an Elk Hair Caddis that I tied using the hair from a bull elk I shot with a bow.

4. It would eliminate the need to shell out two bucks (and more!) for a hook with a bead and some wire.
I hate spending money on something I can do myself. A San Juan Worm or a Beadhead Brassie is a good example of something that takes little time and skill to tie.

5. It would make me a better fly fisher.
When I learned to tie flies, I learned a lot about the feeding habits of trout, when certain flies worked (and when they didn't), and how much of a trout's diet comes from beneath the surface.

> "I COULD BUY A TOP-OF-THE-LINE FLY ROD IF I HAD A 10-SPOT FOR EVERY TIME A FRIEND SAID, 'HERE, I THOUGHT YOU MIGHT WANT THIS FOR FLY TYING MATERIAL.'"

Flies

6 REASONS I (DAVE) DON'T TIE FLIES

I made the decision not to tie. There are consequences to my decision, such as not having the ability to tie a pattern at the river's edge. However, I'd rather buy than tie, and here are some reasons why:

1. We had too many kids.
We ended up with four, and with all their sports and school activities, I can barely get out on the river as it is. A lousy excuse, I know.

2. I also love to hunt.
I've limited my sports to two — fly fishing and hunting. I'd rather fly fish and hunt upland game and waterfowl than spend time in a damp basement under a bright lamp with tiny hooks and peacock herl. Just sayin'.

3. I'd rather write than tie.
In my free time, outside of fly fishing and hunting, I like to write.

4. I'd rather work more than tie.
I've started a couple of small businesses, so I'd probably rather throw my shoulder into landing one more client than spend an evening staring at a vise.

5. The patterns on the market are legion.
I'm grateful for all those who tie flies, and the artistry that I can purchase amazes me.

6. I have too much clutter in my house.
Until the kids all leave (and it looks like it will be a while), we need every square inch of our house for kid stuff.

> "I'D RATHER FLY FISH AND HUNT UPLAND GAME AND WATERFOWL THAN SPEND TIME IN A DAMP BASEMENT UNDER A BRIGHT LAMP WITH TINY HOOKS AND PEACOCK HERL."

Tactics

3 DISCIPLINES TO MASTER SPRING CREEK FLY FISHING

Here are three disciplines for mastering smaller, spring-fed creeks, whose watershed is under the surface of the earth:

1. Casting in and around trees
Fishing the smaller creeks forces the fly fisher to pay attention to his or her cast and focus on precision placement of the fly in the run.

2. Crawling up to a run
If you're catching trout in a spring creek, most likely your knees (and maybe even your elbows) are muddy — because you are stalking the fish.

3. Eliminating false casts
To cast with a minimum of false casts requires endless amounts of practice before you can shoot the line out accurately (or lob it out awkwardly) while hunched over on the edge of stream on your knees.

"IF YOU'RE CATCHING TROUT
IN A SPRING CREEK,
MOST LIKELY YOUR KNEES
(AND MAYBE EVEN YOUR ELBOWS)
ARE MUDDY."

Safety

8 ADDITIONAL SAFE WADING TIPS

There's nothing like crowdsourced content, and these additional eight safe-wading tips come from real fly fishers who posted on our Facebook page or blog:

1. Use wading boots with alternate soles.
Fly fisher Jerry says, "There is no absolute rule regarding wading sole material such as 'only rubber,' 'felt is always best,' 'metal bars grip most,' 'always studs,' etc. That's why I use Korkers and own three different pairs of soles."

2. Wear a belt even if your waders have a built-in Velcro belt.
Fly fisher Bruce says, "Gaining 250 lbs. in three seconds is one of the oddest sensations you'll ever experience! My waders have built in Velcro belts on each side, and I usually fasten them pretty tightly around my waist, but it didn't matter, they still filled up rather instantly. WEAR A GOOD BELT."

3. Wade with a buddy in swift current.

Fly fisher Ray says, "If the water is swift, I wade side by side with one arm around or holding on to my buddy. This provides great stability."

4. Wade with a PFD (personal flotation device).

Fly fisher Norman says, "I have to use the assistance of a cane or staff to walk now and this does make wading a little more difficult. And with the deep, swift rivers we have here in Oregon, I have added a PFD to my equipment list. Especially during steelhead and salmon seasons."

> "WEAR A BELT. GAINING 250 LBS. IN THREE SECONDS IS ONE OF THE ODDEST SENSATIONS YOU'LL EVER EXPERIENCE!"

5. Roll to your side and push up if you fall.

Fly fisher Ed says, "I learned that you will be carried downstream a long ways if you fall and your waders fill. You could drown in waist-high water. I was able to roll on my side and push up in moderately flowing shallow water. If I had been in faster and deeper water, I would not have rolled over and continued at the mercy of the river, hoping to find an overhanging sweeper. Even with a belt, it is not easy to get back on your feet. But it is better."

6. Use studded felt boots for the greased bowling balls.
Fly fisher Jerry says, "I fell a few years ago trying to cross the Gallatin on its greased-bowling-ball rocks. I had a bruise on my hip for over a couple of weeks that looked like a big rib-eye steak. I change soles on my Korkers constantly to match the stream conditions and personally have found studded felt to be the stickiest, even more so than aluminum bars."

7. Aluminum bars stick to the rocks best.
Fly fisher guide Glen says, "I purchased the Patagonia Foot Tractor Wading Boots. Yes, they are expensive, but I value my life. I have owned felt sole, sticky rubber studded, and even studded felt, and nothing compares to the foot tractors. The aluminum bars are like magnets on the rocks. I also always carry a wading staff with me no matter how shallow the water."

8. Work on your core.
Fly fisher Mark says, "Work on your core and leg strength as well as doing balance exercises. It has kept me out of trouble many times. Stay hydrated!"

"WORK ON
YOUR CORE
AND
LEG STRENGTH
AS WELL AS DOING
BALANCE EXERCISES.
IT HAS KEPT ME
OUT OF TROUBLE
MANY TIMES."

Education

7 WAYS TO MAKE THE MOST OF PUBLIC ACCESS

Some say public access is a right, though it may be more of a gift. Either way, fly fishers need to appreciate the access:

1. Don't trash these sites!
Make the effort to pick up after others (and yourself). There's nothing like empty leader packets, plastic grocery bags, and empty beer cans to ruin the mood.

2. Leave the gates as you found them.
If you've been around farms or ranches, you know to shut the gates you open and to leave open the gates that are open!

3. Give livestock a wide berth.
This is common sense. You'll want to give bulls an even wider berth, especially if there is no place to run.

4. Know your legal rights and limits.
In some states, fly fishers can use rivers and streams for recreational purposes up to the ordinary high water mark, even if the water goes through private property. That's the case in Montana. But not in every state.

5. Know how to find access sites.
Most are well marked, though you can purchase maps that show the access points.

6. Walk farther than anyone else.
The farther you walk, the more you'll enjoy less-fished water where the trout have not seen every kind of Beadhead Prince Nymph known to fly fishers.

> "THE FARTHER YOU WALK, THE MORE YOU'LL ENJOY LESS-FISHED WATER."

7. Don't forget the water near the access point.
On a bigger river, most folks in a drift boat are getting ready to take out (when they are upriver from the access point), so they stop fishing about a hundred yards from a fishing access site. And they often don't start fishing until a couple of hundred yards after they put in.

Tactics

5 QUICK TIPS TO CATCHING MORE TROUT ON HOPPERS

Trout often go nuts when hoppers are readily available. That's usually mid-July to mid-August, plus or minus, depending on where you're fishing. Here are five quick tips for success:

1. Be ready!
You'll often get a strike as soon as the hopper hits the water.

2. Size and color matter.
It generally doesn't matter how your hopper imitations are made—whether foam or hair. But the difference between green and brown may make all the difference.

3. Use a smaller fly as a dropper.
Add a dropper or trailer fly by tying on another terrestrial, such as an ant or beetle pattern.

4. Slap 'em and twitch 'em.
You're trying to imitate a hopper falling into the river, not a hopper making a delicate landing. Twitch the hopper to create movement.

5. Aim for the prime time of day.
Prime time is usually mid or late morning to early afternoon. That's when it warms up, and you often see a lot of hopping going on in the grass near the river's edge.

> "SLAP AND TWITCH YOUR HOPPERS TO CREATE MOVEMENT, ESPECIALLY IN SLOWER WATER."

Trips

6 PLANNING TIPS FOR YOUR FLY FISHING TRIP

With some simple preparation and forethought, you can create a memorable fly fishing trip:

1. Try new waters.
If you are heading to an area you've fished before, take an afternoon and fish a new creek.

2. Avoid the two worst seasons.
If you are heading to the American West, fishing the freestone rivers, you may want to avoid two seasons: Blown Out Season (from late April to, often, late June) and the Tourist Season (from mid July to late August). There's always great fly fishing in the summer, but you have to hit it just right.

3. Fish the spawning seasons.
You'll need to be extra careful catching and releasing the fish, but two

great times in the West are spring rainbows before the rivers blow out and the big browns in October.

4. Stay long enough for a banner day.
Often only one day out of a four-day trip ends up being a banner day – a 15 (or more) fish day. So you need to stay long enough to have one.

5. Hire a guide for one of the days.
We like hiring guides, but only for one of the days on a trip. Just budget for the expense. Fishing with a guide will give you some new places to fish (yes, we've gone back later without the guide!) and will provide some coaching. It's a great investment.

6. Build contingencies into your plan.
Nothing is more frustrating than a plan that goes sideways with the weather, especially if you are fishing in early spring or mid-to-late fall. Each day should have two options.

> "WE LIKE HIRING A GUIDE. FISHING WITH A GUIDE WILL GIVE YOU SOME NEW PLACES TO FISH AND WILL PROVIDE SOME COACHING. IT'S A GREAT INVESTMENT."

Inspiration

3 REASONS WHY I (STEVE) FLY FISH

I often get asked, "Why do you fly fish? What do you like about it?" This question typically comes from folks who are dabbling in it or thinking about trying the sport. Here is my answer:

1. I am engaged with the outdoors.
Fly fishing allows me to experience the great outdoors in an interactive way. Rock climbing or hiking doesn't do it for me. I need a bow, a hunting rifle, or a fly rod in hand. Plus, there's nothing like standing in the Madison River in March while the snow is softly falling.

2. I am addicted to the rise.
Fly fishing gives me an adrenaline rush and a sense of satisfaction that most other outdoor sports do not. Only the piercing bugle of a bull elk gives me the sensation I experience when a rainbow rises to attack my hopper pattern.

3. I am connected to the art and skill of the sport.
There is a grace to casting (when done well). And there are endless ways of improving my craft – reading waters, identifying insect hatches, tying flies, maneuvering a drift boat, and casting. Fly fishing is a great sport for life-long learners.

> "FLY FISHING GIVES ME AN ADRENALINE RUSH AND A SENSE OF SATISFACTION THAT MOST OTHER OUTDOOR SPORTS DO NOT."

Trips

10 REASONS TO FISH THE YELLOWSTONE ECOSYSTEM

Here are 10 compelling reasons to cancel all your other vacation plans and fly fish the Greater Yellowstone ecosystem:

1. Your choice of blue-ribbon waters
There's the Yellowstone, the Madison, and the Gallatin — plus a host of other streams like the Lamar, Slough Creek, and the Firehole.

2. The meal at the end of the day
You can wrap up your day on a Montana river with a tender cut of steak at Sir Scott's Oasis in Manhattan or The Rib and Chop House in Livingston or pizza at Colombo's in Bozeman.

3. The spectacular scenery
Nothing compares with the majestic, snow-capped Absaroka-Beartooth Mountains that tower over the Yellowstone River as it flows through Paradise Valley.

4. Biodiversity
You can fly fish big rivers, small streams, spring creeks (in Paradise Valley or the Gallatin Valley), and even lakes (like Henry's Lake or Yellowstone Lake in Yellowstone National Park).

5. Ample access
Thanks to a good supply of public fishing accesses and Montana's "streamside access law," you can fish for miles on any of the big rivers without fear of being kicked off by a landowner or arrested by a game warden.

6. Three-season success
The fishing can be superb in three out of the four seasons, with spring and fall being even better than summer.

7. The prolific hatches
From the fabled Mother's Day caddis hatch to the sure and steady Blue Winged Olive (BWO) and Pale Morning Dun (PMD) hatches, the trout can become ravenous.

8. Wildlife sightings
You'll have a chance to see everything from bald eagles to sand hill cranes to wolves to deer to grizzly bears, and maybe even hear one of nature's most stirring sounds... the bugle of a bull elk.

9. First-class fly shops and guides
The guides in the fly shops in Bozeman, Livingston, Gardiner, and West Yellowstone all know their stuff.

10. Fishing for Yellowstone Cutthroats
It's worth fishing the Yellowstone River inside Yellowstone National Park just to encounter these beautiful fish, many as fat as footballs.

Safety

7 FLY FISHING SAFETY DEVICES

Here are seven fly fishing safety devices or items that are, ultimately, more important than split shot, forceps, or fly floatant. Don't leave home without them:

1. Bear spray
This item is a "must carry" whenever you fly fish in grizzly bear country.

2. Wading belt
This is not a luxury item, yet some beginner fly fishers forget to scrounge through their duffel bag to find it and wear it.

3. First aid kit
You never know when you'll pop a blister or sprain an ankle or embed a hook in your finger.

4. Communications device
Cell phones are nice but unreliable, so we carry two-way radios.

5. Flashlight
With so many compact, lightweight flashlights on the market, you definitely want one in your fly vest or satchel.

> "BEAR SPRAY IS A 'MUST CARRY' ITEM WHENEVER YOU FLY FISH IN GRIZZLY BEAR COUNTRY."

6. Fire starter
If you hike in far enough to fly fish a mountain lake or a remote stretch of river, you might also consider fire starter (a butane lighter and a folded paper towel). Add to that a space blanket (a thin metal-coated sheet that folds up into a pouch the size of your wallet).

7. Water-purification tablets
It's tempting to sate your thirst with the fresh creek water. Don't. You can only purify your water with such tablets or by boiling it for a few minutes.

Inspiration

8 FLY FISHING PERSONALITIES

Fly fishers are a wild and crazy tribe. Here are eight fly fishing personalities that we've encountered on our excursions through the years:

1. Warrior on a Mission
This is the intense, hyper-competitive (most often) male with a testosterone saturated mindset: "I'll do whatever it takes to catch fish." This drives some fly fishers to be rude and inconsiderate of others, even if their intent is pure.

2. Know-It-All
This is the narcissist who simply won't shut up, using every opportunity to tell his or her grand story of large fish and close encounters.

3. Simms Supermodel
This is the pretty boy or pretty girl fly fisher who may fish only once every couple of years but has the best gear that money can buy – and looks perfect wearing it!

4. Golden Boy or Girl
This is the fly fisher who came out of his or her mother's womb with the Midas Touch, the amazing athlete with unbelievable hand-eye coordination. Unfortunately, this does not describe either one of us!

> "DAVE IS A DRAMA KING. STEVE IS A RESTLESS SOUL."

5. Lucky Dog
Unlike the Golden Girl who is genuinely gifted, this person is not so much talented as lucky – often catching the biggest fish. And is annoying to her fly fishing partner.

6. Anxiety-Driven Fisher
This fly fisher is always a bit nervous, feeling as if he or she is not fishing in the right place and thus trying to move you out of your run.

7. Drama King/Queen
This is Dave's fly fishing personality, because he has a penchant for breaking rods and locking keys in the trunk of his car.

8. Restless Soul
This is Steve's fly fishing personality, because he races from run to run, with little patience or thought for others (uh, Dave).

Education

4 WAYS TO ENCOURAGE YOUR KIDS TO FLY FISH

You can lead a child to water, but you can't make him or her fly fish. Here are a few suggestions to help your kids love the sport:

1. Get them on the river early and often.
The time to introduce your kids (or grandkids) to the river is even before they are old enough to fish.

2. Get them hooked on brookies (or sunfish).
Brook trout are a beginner's best friend, since they are often forgiving of sloppy casts. Even bluegills or sunfish will do.

3. Start them on nymph fishing.
Casts do not have to be as precise as in dry fly fishing, and it's easy to teach kids to watch the bobber, er, strike indicator as it floats down a run.

4. Give them a break so they can explore.
Don't be upset if your child loses interest and wants to explore; encourage it! Let your child overturn rocks, chase frogs, pick up sticks, or catch garter snakes (though keep them away from rattlers!).

> "YOU CAN LEAD
> A CHILD TO WATER,
> BUT YOU CAN'T
> MAKE HIM
> OR HER FLY FISH."

Tactics

3 TRUTHS ABOUT THE MOTHER'S DAY CADDIS HATCH

One of the more fabled insect hatches on Montana's great rivers is the so-called Mother's Day caddis hatch. Here are three things you need to know to fish it with success:

1. Mother's Day will be too late.
Don't circle Mother's Day on your calendar and expect to have a banner day, because most years, you will be a couple of weeks too late. The river is usually blown out by then (translation: The river will be too high, too fast, and too muddy for you to catch trout on caddis flies).

2. You will have a hard time seeing your fly.
It's a thrill to see so many caddis on the water and the trout going crazy, but this makes it difficult to find your fly in the mix. Steve has tied some red fibers on the top of his Elk Hair Caddis patterns so

he can spot them. It helps. Also, since your offering is just one of a smorgasbord of options, don't be surprised if your fly gets bypassed. Try again.

3. You may have better success under the surface.
Fishing beneath the surface is often effective before the hatch starts in earnest. Try a Beadhead Red Fox Squirrel nymph as your top fly and a Beadhead Caddis Pupa as your trailer fly.

> "IT'S A THRILL TO SEE
> SO MANY CADDIS
> ON THE WATER
> AND THE TROUT
> GOING CRAZY,
> BUT THIS MAKES IT DIFFICULT
> TO FIND YOUR FLY
> IN THE MIX."

Gear

4 QUESTIONS BEFORE BUYING YOUR FIRST FLY ROD

If you're new to fly fishing, purchasing your first fly rod can be as bewildering as buying a car. And if you ask for recommendations, you'll get eight opinions. Here are four questions to ask before purchasing your first rod:

1. How much do I want to spend?
If you've never fly fished before, a starter rod in the $200 to $300 range will serve you well. Don't be the silly person who lays downs $800 for his or her first rod. Okay, it might not be silly. But it's definitely unnecessary.

2. What length and weight work best for me?
This obviously depends on where you'll be fishing primarily (small spring creeks or larger rivers). If you're fishing for trout in the big western rivers, a nine-foot, six-weight will be a good all-around rod.

You'll be able to sling streamers as well as cast smaller dry flies. For smaller stream fishing, an eight-foot, four-weight works just fine.

3. What type of action is best?
A mid-flex or a medium action, which means that the rod flexes or bends in the middle when you cast your line, is best for a newbie.

> "IF YOU'VE NEVER FLY FISHED BEFORE, A STARTER ROD IN THE $200 TO $300 RANGE WILL SERVE YOU WELL."

4. Which brand is best?
Simply choose a rod that feels right, so any brand like Redington, Temple Fork Outfitters (TFO), St. Croix, or Orvis will work. Some brands like Winston and Sage have a more "premium" perception, but don't start with a brand. Start with what feels right. For you.

Flies

DAVE'S 5 FAVORITE NYMPH AND WET FLY PATTERNS

Here are Dave's go-to nymphs and wet flies when there is no apparent hatch in play:

1. Beadhead Prince Nymph
This is the old trusty go-to nymph. Maybe too trusty. And too common. The fly seems to impersonate the many various mayfly nymphs. Sometimes I use it as my trailer fly in a size #18, especially in the spring when fishing spawning rainbows, if my top fly is an egg pattern.

2. Gold Ribbed Hare's Ear
Another old friend, this nymph looks buggy and seems to imitate both stoneflies and mayflies.

3. Beadhead Pheasant Tail
This is another favorite subsurface attractor pattern for many a fly fisher.

4. Red Copper John
This is a cousin of the brassy, but the color seems to make a difference. At least on some days.

5. San Juan Worm
This wet fly is, well, a worm imitation, and it makes many afternoons on the river less frustrating when used as a dropper.

> "THE RED COPPER JOHN IS A COUSIN OF THE BRASSY, BUT THE COLOR SEEMS TO MAKE A DIFFERENCE. AT LEAST ON SOME DAYS."

Flies

STEVE'S 5 FAVORITE NYMPH AND WET FLY PATTERNS

Here are Steve's five favorite go-to nymphs and wet fly attractor patterns:

1. Beadhead Prince Nymph
This classic seems to imitate both stoneflies and mayflies.

2. Red Copper John
This nymph is often used as a trailer fly or dropper.

3. Red Fox Squirrel Nymph
This works as a caddis pupa imitation.

4. Spawn Egg Pattern
These flies work well for spawning rainbows in the spring and running browns in the fall.

5. San Juan Worm
A worm is a worm, and it works beautifully as a dropper, especially when the water has some color.

> "A WORM IS A WORM, AND THE SAN JUAN WORM WORKS BEAUTIFULLY AS A DROPPER, ESPECIALLY WHEN THE WATER HAS SOME COLOR."

Gear

5 QUESTIONS BEFORE YOU BUY YOUR NEXT PAIR OF WADERS

Each fly fisher sees fly fishing gear differently. But here are five questions to consider before purchasing your next pair of waders:

1. How many days a year do I fly fish?
If you fly fish fewer than 10 to 15 days a year, purchase a middle-of-the-road brand that offers good value at a decent price. If you are a guide or professional fly fisher, you obviously want the best of the best.

2. Is this my only pair of waders?
If so, and you fly fish in temps below 32 degrees Fahrenheit, you may want an insulated pair. Most of us just add layers under our waders.

3. How brand conscious am I?
If you need to wear the most expensive brand because doing so makes you feel good about how you appear to others, by all means, buy the best. We don't.

4. What is my budget?
Find a workhorse pair between $250 and $350, and spend any extra money on your next fly fishing trip.

5. Should I buy waders with boots attached?
No, buy stocking foot waders only. Then purchase a pair of wading boots that maximize your traction in the types of streams you fish. Lots of boot bottoms to choose from: felt, rubber, rubber with studs, and bars.

> "IF YOU FLY FISH FEWER THAN 10 TO 15 DAYS A YEAR, PURCHASE A MIDDLE-OF-THE-ROAD BRAND OF WADERS THAT OFFERS GOOD VALUE, NOT THE TOP BRAND."

# Inspiration

6 ELEMENTS OF A SATISFYING DAY ON THE RIVER

Can't add too much more than this to a great day of fly fishing, no matter where you fly fish:

1. Catching trout
Duh!

2. Catching a lot of trout
Yes! We've had several days when we've caught 20+ trout each. Once, we each caught 40+ trout – really nice ones. The operative word in that sentence is "once."

3. Catching big trout
Yes! Yes! We've had some days on the Madison River in the Beartrap Canyon (in Montana) where we have both landed our share of 18- to 20-inch rainbows.

4. No crowds
You're in the wrong sport if you like company on the river.

5. Great scenery
This is what we love most about fly fishing, especially in the American West. Think golden Aspen leaves, snow-covered peaks, and pine-forested mountainsides.

6. Dinner afterwards
What can be better than three or four thousand calories at a local supper club or chop house after a day of catching huge amounts of huge trout?

> "WHAT CAN BE BETTER THAN THREE OR FOUR THOUSAND CALORIES AT A LOCAL SUPPER CLUB OR CHOP HOUSE AFTER A DAY OF CATCHING HUGE AMOUNTS OF HUGE TROUT?"

Safety

7 MORE SAFE WADING TIPS

You can never be too safe.

Here are seven additional wading tips from fly fishers who posted their suggestions to our Facebook page or web site:

1. Switch to waist waders.
Fly fisher Dave says, "I switched to waist waders a few years ago, mainly to resist the temptation to wade too deep."

2. Face upstream when you cross.
Fly fisher Neil says, "Always face upstream when crossing so you don't get your feet swept out from under you."

Fly fisher Ryan says, "Walking downstream is considered to be wrong because it's much easier to get your feet swept out."

Fly fisher Chris says, "Facing downstream when wading in deeper water can get your torso pushed over faster than your feet can keep up."

3. Leg position matters in heavy water.
Fly fisher Matt says, "Standing upstream legs out like a sumo is bad – double the current and no stability. Front leg upstream, with the rear leg tucked into the turbulent flow allows weight shifting from front to rear. Front foot acts as a probe, rear foot follows."

4. Close all your pockets.
Fly fisher Frank says, "Make sure all your pockets are closed shut."

5. Take a water safety class.
Fly fisher Pepe says, "Take a water safety course. As a fisher and a paddler, I think it would help."

6. Focus on leg technique.
Fly fisher Matt says, "Things that actually matter like keeping your legs parallel to the current (front leg breaks the current and the rear leg is facing half the current) are crucial. Technique matters."

7. Don't get tunnel vision.
Fly fisher Ryan says, "Don't get tunnel vision, standing there focused on your fly or casting for too long. Look around every now and then. Bears are often looking for the same fish you are, and don't appreciate your poaching their quarry. Be aware!"

> "FLY FISHER FRANK SAYS, 'MAKE SURE ALL YOUR POCKETS ARE CLOSED SHUT.'"

# Safety

5 WILD ANIMALS TO OBSERVE AT A DISTANCE

Running into wildlife while on the river is one of the great wonders of fly fishing. Here are five you would be better off enjoying at a distance:

1. Wolves
In Yellowstone Park, a wolf sauntered down a ridge and lay down directly across the Yellowstone River from us while we fly fished. We were not scared, but being watched felt eerie. After a few minutes, the wolf returned to the timber.

2. Bison
Also in Yellowstone Park, a curious bull bison walked up to us within 30 yards while we hiked back to the trailhead after a day of fly fishing. We had a few anxious moments until he finally turned and sauntered up the ridge.

3. Grizzly Bears
Thankfully, we've never run into a grizzly while fly fishing in Yellowstone Park, though we have seen bear tracks on the trail to a favorite run near Gardiner, Montana. We've had friends who have been attacked by grizzlies, though, so we're always cautious and carry bear spray.

> "THANKFULLY, WE'VE NEVER RUN INTO A GRIZZLY WHILE FLY FISHING IN YELLOWSTONE PARK, THOUGH WE HAVE SEEN BEAR TRACKS ON THE TRAIL TO A FAVORITE RUN."

4. Rattlesnakes
Thankfully, we've had no close encounters. Steve used to see rattlers along the Madison River when he lived in Montana.

5. Moose
Nothing is more dangerous than a cow that is unhappy that you stumbled upon her and her calf.

Safety

5 PRECAUTIONS TO TAKE WHILE FLY FISHING

It all depends on where you fish, but here are several precautions to keep in mind as you head out to the river:

1. Carry bear spray.
You can't carry bear spray on a plane, and it expires after several years. But it's worth the investment even if you are in bear country for only a few days. Obviously, if you don't fish where there are grizzly bears, you have no worries.

2. Use two-way radios.
They beat cell phones for coverage, though they may have limited range.

3. Watch out for venomous snakes.
If you get bit, position the area of the bite above your heart, if possible. And don't "suck the venom out of the bite." That's old school. And

dead wrong. The use of snakebite kits is debated. The medical experts we've consulted frown on them.

4. Stay in view of your partner.
Especially if you're in bear country, it's important to check in with and keep in view of your fly fishing buddy. Besides, you never know when one of you might slip and fall.

> "IT'S IMPORTANT TO CHECK IN WITH AND KEEP IN VIEW OF YOUR FLY FISHING BUDDY. YOU NEVER KNOW WHEN ONE OF YOU MIGHT SLIP AND FALL."

5. Be aware of your surroundings.
This sounds like advice for when you're walking in a bad Chicago neighborhood late at night, but it also applies to fly fishing in the great outdoors. Weather can change quickly. Predators can appear out of nowhere.

Tactics

12 SIMPLE FLY FISHING HACKS

A hack is a shortcut or a trick, a way of doing something more quickly or efficiently — or simply.

Here are 12 (of many possible) hacks:

1. Double over your fly line (not your leader) to make a small loop and thread it through the guides.
When threading your line through your guides, don't use the leader (like Steve did the first few times he fly fished!); instead, use the fly line.

2. Use a candle to wax your rod ferrules.
It makes it so much easier to insert one section of your rod into the next. And to pull each section apart.

3. Throw a piece of a carpet in your trunk or truck.
You'll appreciate it when you're putting on your waders when there's snow or gravel on the ground. An old rug works great, too.

4. Wet your leader knot before you tighten it.
If you don't, the friction when tightening the knot may weaken the monofilament. Spit works beautifully.

5. Bring a garbage bag for your wet stuff.
It creates separation between your dry world and wet world. And it contains the odor, too!

6. Use the river as a visual backdrop for the knot that you're trying to tie.
Doing so makes the monofilament seem backlit – and much easier to thread.

7. Use polarized sunglasses.
They create the contrast when looking at the river. They allow you to see more clearly. Hey, there are three trout beside that rock!

8. Stand at the river's edge for a minute before you step into it.
This may not be so much a hack as common sense. There may be some trout rising near the bank.

9. Position your rod to a 45° angle when fighting the fish.
Doing so puts the pressure on the mid section and makes the rod work for you. Plus, you'll avoid breaking the tip if you're fighting a big one.

10. Pull the fish to the side when bringing it in.
Pulling the fish sideways tires it out and allows you to bring it in more quickly – and thus release it more quickly.

11. Fly fish the first 100 yards up where drift boats take out or the first 100 yards where they put in.
Often fly fishers don't start fishing immediately or stop fishing as they get ready to complete their trip.

12. Bring a fresh pair of socks.
A change of socks is a beautiful thing after a hard day of hiking and fishing.

Tactics

4 PRACTICES TO BREAK OUT OF A FLY FISHING SLUMP

One parallel between baseball and fly fishing is the slump. To break out, we suggest four practices:

1. Just keep fishing.
Baseball players hit their way out of a slump, and fly fishers need to just keep plugging away. One day, it all starts to change.

2. Go with a pro.
That may mean fly fishing with someone better than you or simply hiring a guide for a day or two.

3. Go back to school.
You may want to take a fly casting or fly tying class. Or, depending

on your learning style, work your way through a video series or book. There are so many opportunities to improve your knowledge and skills. You may want to start with one skill that you want to improve. For example, one idea is to work on your roll cast.

4. Try something new.
Sometimes you simply need to switch it up by fishing new waters or during another time of the year. Or treating yourself to a new fly rod (yea!).

"BASEBALL PLAYERS HIT THEIR WAY OUT OF A SLUMP, AND FLY FISHERS NEED TO JUST KEEP PLUGGING AWAY."

Safety

5 COMMON FLY FISHING DANGERS

What is so obvious is often easiest to overlook. Here are five dangers that fly fishers should never take lightly:

1. Falling
Falling down an incline or slipping on a boulder and twisting your ankle may be life-threatening. Even if it's not, a fall can end a day of fly fishing. It could also be expensive. Steve was on the return hike from fly fishing a high mountain lake when he witnessed a helicopter rescuing a hiker with a broken ankle. Wonder what the bill was for that?

2. Lightning
Be sure to move away from water, place your fly rod flat on the ground, make yourself small (crouch in a ditch), and stay away from big structures.

3. Hypothermia
This occurs when your body loses heat faster than it can produce it.

Remove wet clothing, cover the person with blankets, provide warm beverages, and share body heat (skin to skin is best), if desperate.

4. Drowning
Limit how deep you will go in swift water, use the right soles for your wading boots, add a wading staff to your must-have gear, and use two wading belts (mid-section and chest high).

5. Wildlife
Give bison and moose a wide berth, carry bear spray, and watch for rattlesnakes.

> "FALLING DOWN AN INCLINE OR SLIPPING ON A BOULDER AND TWISTING YOUR ANKLE MAY BE LIFE-THREATENING. EVEN IF IT'S NOT, A FALL CAN END A DAY OF FLY FISHING."

Inspiration

5 DISCIPLINES TO FLY FISH MORE

It may seem a counterintuitive concept that fly fishing needs to be a priority, but as life grows more complex, it really does. Here are five disciplines that will help get you out on the river more often:

1. Limit your hobbies.
There's probably not enough time to be great at golf – and fly fishing. That might explain why there is little overlap between fly fishers and golfers.

2. Put it on your calendar.
Sounds simple enough, but once the time has been budgeted, it's harder to kick the can down the road.

3. Find a fly fishing buddy.
This is probably harder than it sounds if you're just starting out, but a buddy tends to hold you accountable to get out on the river.

4. Make the most of small windows of time.
Sometimes less is all you have, so take the small amount of time and get out on the river. For those of you who live within an hour of a river, go with your gut and jump in your truck, even if you have only a couple hours. You don't need large chunks of time.

5. Take chunks of time off.
This is the opposite of the previous point, but three or four days at a crack often work better in certain seasons of life. We've also found it difficult to budget time to fly fish on a family vacation.

> "THERE'S PROBABLY
> NOT
> ENOUGH TIME
> IN YOUR LIFE
> TO BE GREAT
> AT GOLF — AND
> FLY FISHING."

Tactics

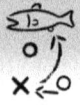

4 WAYS TO MAKE FLY FISHING SIMPLE

If you're just starting out, here are some ways to minimize complexity and keep fly fishing simple:

1. Knots
The two we use most are the improved clinch knot and the surgeons' knot (or some form of it).

2. Leaders
Begin with 5x, and 6x leaders. If you are throwing streamers, go with 3x.

3. Flies
Start with an Elk Hair Caddis and a Parachute Adams for dries (in a couple of sizes), and a Beadhead Prince Nymph or Pheasant Tail, the Red Copper John, and the San Juan Worm for wet flies. And you can never go wrong with a Woolly Bugger, the streamer of champions!

4. Casting
Just get good at mending your line — flipping the middle section of your rod upstream. Later, you can learn how to mend your line in air (by writing the letter "C" with your rod tip), right before the fly lands on the water.

"THE TWO KNOTS WE USE MOST ARE THE IMPROVED CLINCH KNOT AND THE SURGEONS' KNOT."

Inspiration

3 TAKEAWAYS FROM "A RIVER RUNS THROUGH IT"

Whether you read the book or watch the movie, there are some themes that may resonate with you. They do with us, especially the deep family ties.

1. Sometimes those who are closest to us are the hardest to understand.
This is one of the saddest but most profound truths of family life, especially when there is great pain in the relationship. As Norman Maclean wrote, "It is those we live with and love and should know who elude us."

2. You can love someone completely without completely understanding him or her.
Fly fishing brings together family members even when there is conflict or misunderstanding.

3. Fly fishing stirs our inconsolable longing, a desire for something beyond ourselves.
The sport evokes peacefulness and a deep sense of satisfaction, mingled with a poignant ache or sadness, what British writer C.S. Lewis called the "inconsolable longing." We affirm Norman Maclean's final line in his novella: "I am haunted by waters."

> "WE AFFIRM NORMAN MACLEAN'S FINAL LINE IN HIS NOVELLA: 'I AM HAUNTED BY WATERS.'"

Trips

5 TIPS WHEN FISHING THE YELLOWSTONE ECOSYSTEM

We think every fly fisher should experience the blue-ribbon rivers and streams of the Yellowstone Ecosystem at least once. But it's a vast country, with almost unlimited places to fish. Here are some tips to help you make the most of your trip:

1. Where to Fish
- Yellowstone River, the longest free-flowing undammed waterway in the lower 48 states, which can be floated or waded.
- Madison River, outside Yellowstone National Park and beyond Hebgen and Quake Lake, with three main stretches: The Upper Madison, The Beartrap, and the Lower Madison.
- Gallatin River, which is closer to Bozeman, MT, so there is more fly fishing pressure on it.
- Spring Creeks in Paradise Valley (Nelson's, Armstrong's, and DePuys), which all have a daily rod fee.

- Other rivers and streams include those inside Yellowstone National Park – the Yellowstone, Slough Creek, the Lamar, the Firehole, and Madison, plus smaller streams such as Taylor Fork and Fan Creek.

2. When to Fish
- Spring. Rainbows spawning on the Madison late March, early April; fabled Mother's Day caddis hatch hits about the time the rivers blow out; weather is always a wild card in spring.
- Summer. May and June tend to be predictably good only on spring creeks, though you can find caddis hatches; water drops in July, but hoppers can be good in August.
- Fall. Late September and October can be great as the browns start to run, and with fewer fly fishers on the rivers, everything improves!

> "THE YELLOWSTONE ECOSYSTEM IS A VAST COUNTRY, WITH ALMOST UNLIMITED PLACES TO FISH."

3. Where to Stay
- Bozeman – for all-around accessibility. It's about 25 miles to Yellowstone River in Livingston to the east, and about that far to the Lower Madison to the west. The Gallatin River is nearby, too.
- West Yellowstone is a great place to stay if you're going to fish the Madison or the Firehole in the Park.
- Livingston is another option if you plan to fish the Yellowstone in Paradise Valley or the Gardner or the Yellowstone in the Park.

4. Fly Shops
- Bozeman: Fins & Feathers; Montana Troutfitters; and The River's Edge.
- Livingston: Dan Bailey's and George Anderson's Yellowstone Angler.
- West Yellowstone: Craig Mathews Blue Ribbon Flies; Bob Jacklin's Fly Shop; and Bud Lilly's.
- Gardiner: Park's Fly Shop.

5. Eateries (this will make or break your trip)
- Bozeman area: Sir Scott's Oasis (Manhattan); Colombo's Pizza; Ted's Montana Grill (okay, a chain); Burger Bob's (Sorry, we're open!); MacKenzie River Pizza; Sandwiches from the Pickle Barrel; and Montana Ale Works.
- Livingston: Rib and Chop House and Chico Hot Springs (south of Livingston in Paradise Valley)
- Gallatin Canyon: Lone Mountain Guest Ranch (lunch) and Corral Bar and Steakhouse (on highway 191 south of Big Sky Ski Resort).
- Yellowstone National Park. Fishing Bridge General Store.

"WE THINK EVERY
FLY FISHER
SHOULD EXPERIENCE
THE BLUE-RIBBON
RIVERS
AND
STREAMS OF THE
YELLOWSTONE
ECOSYSTEM
AT LEAST ONCE."

Flies

4 REMINDERS BEFORE YOU FISH A HATCH

Here are four quick ideas before fishing a hatch:

1. Ask the fly shop monkeys before you hit the river.
You don't need to become an entomologist, but talk to the folks at your local fly shop to know what's rising. Become familiar with the most common insects and when they hatch.

2. Try a different size before you switch patterns.
Fishing in a snowstorm a few years ago, we began catching rainbows when we switched from a size #14 to a size #18 Parachute Adams. Same fly pattern, different size.

3. Consider fishing under the surface (with emergers).
Sometimes, when you see a trout roll, it is not feeding on the surface but on emergers just beneath the film. Use a dropper with your dry fly or move to nymph fishing.

4. Fish a fly you can see.
When there is a blizzard of bugs on the water, you'll appreciate the white post of a parachute pattern or some colored fibers on the top of the fly.

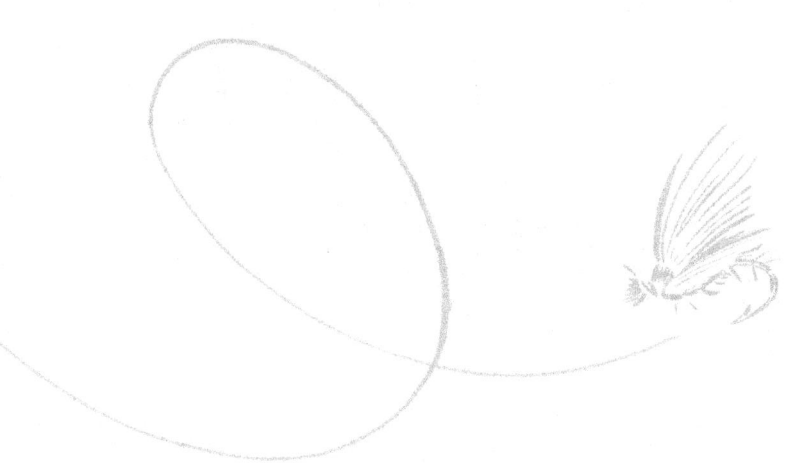

"YOU DON'T NEED TO BECOME
AN ENTOMOLOGIST,
BUT TALK TO THE FOLKS
AT YOUR LOCAL FLY SHOP
TO
KNOW WHAT'S RISING."

Trips

5 LESSONS FROM A RECENT FLY FISHING TRIP

It seems we need to relearn these every time we take a fly-fishing trip:

1. Fish look for the maximum amount of calories with the least amount of effort.
We watched a Trico hatch for an hour or so with no risers, but when we began tossing hoppers, the fish went nuts. Hoppers were a bigger morsel!

2. You're only as good as the water you fish!
One day we caught hardly any, the next day we each landed more than 40 trout each (this is not an apocryphal story).

3. Avoid drag.
Why do we have to relearn this again and again and again?

4. If at first you don't succeed, try something different.
On the Yellowstone, we started catching cutthroat trout when we added more weight to our nymph rigs. We needed to get the nymph closer to the bottom of the run.

5. Nature is not always tranquil.
Dave watched a mink steal a baby duck from a nest within three yards of where he was crouched along the river. Dave backed away very slowly.

> "FISH LOOK FOR THE MAXIMUM AMOUNT OF CALORIES WITH THE LEAST AMOUNT OF EFFORT."

Inspiration

8 STUPID THINGS WE'VE DONE WHILE FLY FISHING

Some days you just have to wonder why we're such idiots:

1. Steve leaves his fly rod on the top of the truck in the parking lot.
He regretted his lack of mindfulness about a mile into the hike to the river, and fortunately, it was still there. But the delay meant that another fly fisher beat us to the spot we wanted to fish.

2. Dave snaps the tip off his rod four miles into the back country of Yellowstone National Park.
He reminds Steve that he still figured out a way to out-fish him that day.

3. Steve takes his eight-year-old brother on a dangerous hike around Upper Two Medicine Lake near Glacier National Park.
The fishing always looks better on the other side of the lake. This

notion causes anglers (like Steve) to lose their common sense. "It doesn't look too steep," Steve thinks, as he fears for their lives while peering into the abyss of the lake.

4. Now Dave leaves his rod on the top of the truck.
This time, the fly rod disappears for good into the wind as Steve and Dave drive off oblivious to Dave's mistake. However, all is well that ends well. Dave gets a new fly rod out of the deal.

5. Dave floats down the Yellowstone while wading on the river's greased cannonballs.
He's lucky to be alive, though this time he eventually found his fly rod. Steve may or may not have laughed as Dave was splashing in the river.

6. Dave leaves the car door open while fly fishing in Wisconsin's Driftless.
It's one thing to lock the doors, and it's quite another to return after three hours of fly fishing and realize that your driver's side door was never closed. Nothing stolen.

7. Dave locks his keys in his car on a back country road near the Scapegoat Wilderness in Montana.
There's nothing like flagging down a rancher who drives by and then hearing the sound of his screwdriver and hammer punching the lock out on the trunk of your mint-condition 1971 Chevy Nova.

8. Steve and Dave walk willfully too close to a herd of bison while returning from a day on the river near dark.
When the bull gets curious and begins to saunter closer to them, they utter a prayer and make a beeline for the river in case they need to float down the Yellowstone the rest of the way home. The bull finally turns away in disgust.

Gear

9 ITEMS TO WEATHER THE WEATHER

Weather is always a factor when fly fishing, and being prepared is basic to safety and enjoyment:

1. Waders
Waders are often unnecessary in summer. But they feel awesome in mid-summer when the temp has plummeted after a squall. If we're hiking a ways into the back country, we'll often take them along, even if it's warm.

2. Rain Gear
This is as basic as it gets. If you are in the outdoors, spend the money on good rain gear. Don't go cheap. If you're already wearing waders, all you need is a good rain jacket.

3. Layers
Folks have preached this for years, but it's an important reminder

to wear layers if you plan to hike into a river or lake. You can add or subtract as the weather dictates.

4. Wool Cap or Gore-Tex Hat
Heat escapes quickly through the top of one's head, and the sun is merciless.

5. Gloves
In the spring when the snow squall hits while you're standing in waist-deep water, your fingers will thank you.

6. Hot Chocolate and Coffee
Nothing beats a steaming cup of coffee (or hot chocolate for anglers like Steve who love the smell of coffee but not the taste), unless your partner brought the only thermos and he won't share.

7. Water
The American College of Sports Medicine recommends drinking water during exercise as well as before and after to promote proper hydration and in order to replace water loss through sweating at a similar rate to that at which it is lost. Duh!

8. Matches and a Flashlight
If you're fishing in the American West and hiking into a lake or river, you'll definitely want to bring along some matches and a small flashlight. A folded paper towel will serve as firestarter.

9. Neck Gator
This is a pullover for your head that covers your neck, forehead, and face from the sun. This is way better than sunscreen.

"SPEND THE MONEY ON GOOD RAIN GEAR. DON'T GO CHEAP."

Trips

3 WAYS TO TRACK YOUR ADVENTURES

The memories of great days on the water fade and blur with time. One solution is to keep track of your fly fishing adventures. Here are three simple (and somewhat obvious) ideas to maintain a record:

1. Take plenty of photos.
The cliché "a picture is worth a thousand words" is eternal. Be sure also to record video of your fly fishing partner as he or she makes a dreadful cast.

2. Keep a fly fishing journal.
Sometimes, though, a word is worth a thousand pictures, so consider a fly fishing journal, a great way to relive your memorable days on the river. As we learn fly fishing hacks, or collect intel on new waters, we add them to our journals.

3. Create a social media footprint.
This is not for everybody, but Facebook, Twitter, Google Plus, and Instagram are free, of course, and many hosted blogs like WordPress are also free. Instagram is the favorite of many fly fishers who want to brag about their fish.

> "A WORD IS WORTH
> A THOUSAND PICTURES,
> SO CONSIDER
> A FLY FISHING JOURNAL,
> A GREAT WAY TO RELIVE
> YOUR MEMORABLE DAYS
> ON THE RIVER."

Flies

8 TIPS TO START "MOUSING"

Okay, so this isn't a fly. It's an imitation of a rodent, but slinging a size #6 mouse pattern may just connect you with a monster brown. Here are eight tips to get started:

1. Buy a mouse pattern.
Try a size #6 to start, but don't leave the pattern on your desk at home, or you might freak out your kids.

2. Choose a moonless night.
Or an early moonless morning, say 4:30 or so.

3. Snip an old 5x or 6x leader to 3x.
Sure, you could buy a new 3x leader for this, but why? You'll want a shorter leader anyway.

4. Scout the waters.
You will likely want to be familiar with the stretch of river you're fishing, including where you think the big boys (and girls) will be feeding.

5. Slap the mouse on the edge of the stream.
No, don't slap your line on the water, slap the mouse on the water.

6. Strip the mouse back in inch-long strips.
Or whatever works.

> "DON'T LOSE PATIENCE;
> STAY WITH IT
> UNTIL
> A MONSTER BROWN
> MAKES YOUR NIGHT."

7. Resist the urge to stop stripping as you near the end.
We've all had trout hit at the last possible moment.

8. Rinse and repeat.
Don't lose patience; stay with it until a monster brown makes your night.

Inspiration

OUR 6 FAVORITE OUTDOOR AUTHORS

It's impossible to fly fish 24/7, especially for us, since we live with 10 million of our friends in the Chicago area. So we often go outdoors in our mind.

Here are six of our favorite authors who bring the outdoors indoors:

1. Bud Lilly
Bud Lilly's Guide to Fly Fishing the New West is a classic, especially the part where he writes about a typical conversation with fly fishers when he owned a fly shop in West Yellowstone, Montana.

2. Norman Maclean
Okay, we had to include him, since we both revisit his novella *A River Runs Through It* at least once a year. This was a personal favorite of ours long before the movie was released.

3. Rick Bass
This is one of Dave's favorite writers, and his book about one of his hunting dogs "Colter" will make you laugh and cry.

4. Ernest Hemingway
Ernest embodied the definition of "tortured soul," but his short story *Big Two-Hearted River* is a must-read for any fly fisher.

5. Wallace Stegner
Stegner is a bit more literary, but his Pulitzer prize-winning *Angle of Repose* weaves a tragic story set in the American West.

6. Ivan Doig
Doig was born in a cabin just up the valley from where Steve pastored a church for 14 years, and his classic, *This House of Sky*, narrates his early years in Montana.

> "ERNEST HEMINGWAY EMBODIED THE DEFINITION OF 'TORTURED SOUL,' BUT HIS SHORT STORY 'BIG TWO-HEARTED RIVER' IS A MUST-READ FOR ANY FLY FISHER."

THE 3 KINDS OF RIVERS YOU'LL FLY FISH

Every part of the world boasts different kinds of water, with different insects and with varying carrying capacity for trout. Here are three general categories of rivers you will likely fish:

1. Freestone Rivers
Common in the American West, their major watershed is on the surface of the land and thus subject to flood, with wildly swinging temperatures and water depths. Think the Yellowstone or the Upper Madison in Montana. The variance in water conditions means you'll have some days that are unforgettable and other days that are forgettable.

2. Spring Creeks
With their watersheds largely underground, these streams tend to be more uniform in temperature and more uniform in water flow throughout the year. Think Nelson's or Armstrong's Spring Creeks south

of Livingston, Montana, or the spring creeks in the Driftless area of southeastern Minnesota or southwestern Wisconsin. The crystal clarity of these creeks and the abundance of aquatic insects they produce mean that trout will be more selective. Stealth mode is a must.

3. Tailwaters
Essentially tailwaters have their watersheds under a lake formed by a dam, and thus tend to have more even water flows, more like a spring creek. The damming of the American West has created many tailwater fisheries. Think the Owyhee River in eastern Oregon. Tailwaters are often a bit off-color, so the trout may not spook as easily as they do in a spring creek.

> "WITH THEIR WATERSHEDS LARGELY UNDERGROUND, SPRING CREEKS TEND TO BE MORE UNIFORM IN TEMPERATURE AND MORE UNIFORM IN WATER FLOW THROUGHOUT THE YEAR."

Tactics

8 ADJUSTMENTS TO MAKE FOR SPRING CREEKS

We once interviewed Gary Borger (garyborger.com), fly fisher extraordinaire and hero of ours, and he made it pretty clear why those who have fly fished primarily in the American West in freestone rivers struggle a bit on spring creeks.

Here are eight adjustments you will need to make to catch fish in spring creeks:

1. Your attitude
You need to view spring creeks as a challenge, since you won't be ripping out 30 fish in a couple of hours.

2. Your tackle
You will need to refine your tackle, and you may need to drop to a 6x or 7x leader; use the lightest line and heaviest tippet that you possibly can.

3. Your fly presentation
Trout may have more opportunity to look at your fly because of the clear water, and with lots of insects from which to choose, they'll be picky.

4. Your playing of the fish
With more refined tackle, such as finer leaders, and (in some spring creeks) bigger trout, you'll need more sophistication in how you play the fish.

5. Your visibility
Make sure you stay off the horizon line, and crawl on your hands and knees to the runs.

6. Your clothing
Make sure your clothing blends in with the area around the stream, and wear absolutely no brightly colored outerwear.

7. Your casting
It's easier to cast over and spook trout in smaller spring creeks, so absolutely no false casting.

8. Your approach to the stream
Spend more time stalking the fish. You simply cannot walk up to a run and begin casting. You'll need to keep your profile low and crawl up to the run on your hands and knees.

> "TO FISH SPRING CREEKS SUCCESSFULLY, YOU'LL NEED TO REFINE YOUR TACKLE."

Trips

OUR 6 FAVORITE EATERIES IN THE YELLOWSTONE ECOSYSTEM

There's nothing like a great dinner after a great day on the river.

If you plan to fish anywhere near Bozeman, Montana, you'll want to make sure you hit these fine establishments before or after you fish:

1. Sir Scott's Oasis (Manhattan, MT)
This doesn't look like much from the outside, but it is the one place you must patronize when you fly fish near Bozeman, Montana. It's a meat and potatoes kind of place. And you just might see an NFL coach or a country music star eating there (we have).

2. Rib and Chop House (Livingston, MT)
This is another outstanding place if you like beef, and the Yellowstone River flows right by the town.

3. Colombos (Bozeman, MT)

Yes, we are from Chicago, with the best stuffed pizza in the world, but we dig this tiny pizza joint near the campus of Montana State University.

4. Burger Bob's (Bozeman, MT)

This local burger joint in Bozeman has a memorable sign on the front window: "Sorry, we're open." But we're never sorry after eating their burgers and fries.

5. Chico Hot Springs (Paradise Valley, MT)

This is located in Paradise Valley between Livingston, Montana, and Gardiner, Montana, the north entrance to Yellowstone Park. It's a quasi-resort, and the food at the restaurant is outstanding.

6. The General Store (near Fishing Bridge in Yellowstone National Park)

Once we were starving (having not eaten for a couple of hours!) and the burgers at this sleepy grill made us super happy. It has a retro feel and good food.

Gear

5 QUESTIONS BEFORE YOU SET UP YOUR NEW REEL

If you're new to fly fishing, or you simply have never set up an extra reel with line, here are five questions to make sure you get it right the first time:

1. Which hand will you use to reel in the line?
There's no right answer. Some right-handed fly fishers cast with their right hand and crank with their left. And some left-handed fishers cast with their left and crank with their left. Other right-handed fly fishers cast with their right and then when they catch a fish, they switch hands with the rod and crank with the right. Same with left-handers.

2. How should the drag be set?
It should be tight enough so that the fish on the other end feels some resistance as it fights, but not so tight that a sudden move by the fish snaps your tippet at its weakest point.

3. What kind of backing should I use?
Yes, you need backing. There are several reasons you want to put on backing before you add your fly line, including more line if you catch Moby Dick and it makes a run for it. We use Dacron backing, but some anglers also like gel-spun polyester.

4. What pound strength should I use for backing?
Depends on the size of fish you're after. We generally use 20-pound strength for freshwater fishing, but go to 30 if you have a saltwater outfit. And if you're fishing for small brookies and rainbows mostly, 12-pound strength should work.

5. What kinds of knots should I use to tie on the backing?
You'll need to tie on the backing to the reel, and then you'll need to tie the backing to the fly line. Orvis has a great little book called *The Orvis Pocket Guide to Leaders, Knots, and Tippet*, and it recommends the Arbor Knot for the backing-to-reel knot and the Nail Knot for the backing-to-fly line knot. Better yet, the folks at your local fly shop will generally tie it on for free if you buy your fly line there.

> "DRAG SHOULD BE SET TIGHT ENOUGH SO THAT THE FISH ON THE OTHER END FEELS SOME RESISTANCE AS IT FIGHTS."

Safety

8 SMART REACTIONS WHEN YOU FALL INTO THE RIVER

It's impossible to know how you're going to react when you feel the icy water pour over the top of your waders and you shoot down the river. Here are some smart reactions, with a tip of the hat to Steve's good friend, Duane Dunham, of Portland, Oregon:

1. Don't panic.
Or, rather, panic for a split second and then think rationally. Easy to say while we are all warm and dry and sipping a latte.

2. Don't attempt to stand up too quickly.
Wait until you are in knee-deep water.

3. Never fight the current.
Let it take you, but angle toward shore. Otherwise, you'll become exhausted.

4. Take a breath and push off the bottom toward shore.
If you are in deep water and do this enough times, you'll get there.

5. Keep your feet down stream.
If you are out of control and headed downstream, this will help you avoid hitting your head on a rock.

> "DON'T ATTEMPT TO STAND UP
> TOO QUICKLY
> WHEN YOU FALL
> INTO THE RIVER."

6. Stay in a semi-sitting position as you shoot down the river.
This may be the most important tip! It makes it easier to keep your feet down stream and your head above water.

7. Let go of your fly rod.
This is for emergency situations. Doing so allows you to use both hands to stroke towards shore.

8. Don't laugh at your fly fishing partner.
Dave hopes Steve reads this book and applies this principle.

Tactics

5 TRUTHS WHEN FISHING DRY FLIES AFTER DARK

There are times to fly fish past dark, especially during the dog days of summer. Here are some basic truths about after-dark fishing:

1. Browns like to feed in darkness.
This is common knowledge, but a good reminder: Brown trout come out of their lairs when the day is dying in the west. Don't quit too soon.

2. The white post on a tiny Parachute Adams makes it stand out.
You can see the white post easily enough as long as there is a little light in the sky. The tan wing of an Elk Hair Caddis is easy to spot, too, in waning light.

3. Assume that any rise in the vicinity of your fly is a strike.
This is a basic defense tactic when the ambient light isn't enough to spot your dry fly as it floats down the current.

4. Go with shorter casts.
It's easier to see your fly and to control your line as the darkness takes over. Also, it will keep you from snagging a rock or a branch on the other side of the bank – a lesson Steve has still not learned!

5. A flashlight can save the day, er, the night.
After you snag your line because you didn't adhere to point #4, you will be forced to try to thread a 6x tippet through the eyelet of a size #18 hook. Good luck with that if you don't have a flashlight. Or if your cell phone is back at the truck.

> "WHEN FISHING NEAR DARK, ASSUME THAT ANY RISE IN THE VICINITY OF YOUR FLY IS A STRIKE."

Tactics

7 SPOTS TO CAST YOUR DRY FLY

If you are new to fly fishing, here are the best spots to cast your dry fly:

1. Where the trout are rising
Scan the surface for the subtle rises. It is easy to miss rising fish. The largest trout often make the smallest ripple. Their snouts barely break the surface.

2. Where you are about to wade
Fly fishing legend Gary Borger says, "Fish it before you wade it." The best spot might be the water through which you need to wade to get to the next best spot.

3. Where the drift boats fish
Fly fishers in drift boats do not cast to the middle of the river. They typically cast to the banks — right where you are standing. If you're fishing a large river, think of the first eight to 10 feet from the bank as a small stream.

4. The head of a pool or run
This is the place where fast moving water (a riffle) rushes into a slower, deeper section of current. Sometimes, the riffle empties into a pool.

5. In the foam line of a run
Sometimes, the trout are below the riffle in the current itself. These runs can be short or long. Watch for moving foam and bubbles. This is the food line!

6. The shallow water at the side or the tail end of a run
You won't always find trout in these places, because they offer minimal protection from predators. But they are great feeding spots for trout when the insect hatches are in full force. Often, the more gentle side of a "seam" (the imaginary dividing line between fast moving current and slow water) is a great place to cast a dry fly.

7. Near a rock
Some rivers – or stretches of rivers – do not have pronounced runs. Rather, they have a steady flow and depth from one bank to another. Look for big rocks. We've caught trout in front of, behind, and beside big rocks.

> "OFTEN, THE MORE GENTLE SIDE OF A 'SEAM' IS A GREAT PLACE TO CAST A DRY FLY."

Tactics

4 NOTES ON FLY FISHING KNOTS

Here are some notes on knots to give you some knot know-how. If you're new to fly fishing, tying your tippet to your fly or (worse) tying your tippet to a leader can seem daunting. And time consuming. And frustrating.

Here a few notes that will simplify the process and get you fly fishing:

1. Try this at home.
Don't wait until you're on the bank of the Lochsa or the Hoosic for your inaugural attempt at securing your fly to a tippet with a knot. Try this at home. If trying to learn a new knot, use a small rope or piece of yarn or string. Tie the knot onto a key ring or an eye bolt. Then, you can graduate to tying actual monofilament (which has a mind of its own) onto an actual eye of a hook. Practice may not make perfect, but practice does make progress.

2. Learn two or three basic knots.
You can get away with two knots — one for tying your fly to your tippet, and the other for tying tippet to your leader.

The first knot is the improved clinch knot. You will use this to tie your tippet (or the end of your leader) to your fly. Use eight turns rather than the recommended five. The second is the surgeon's loop. It's quicker to tie than an improved clinch knot, so it's a bit easier when your hands are cold. The only drawback is that you'll waste more material.

To see a video on how to tie both knots, simply search the web with the phrases "improved clinch knot" and "surgeon's loop."

3. Use the river as background.
One of the frustrations you'll face when you try to tie a knot is seeing the tiny loop(s) you've created and seeing the tiny tag end you're trying to push through the loop(s). Use the river as a backdrop. It works surprisingly well.

4. Moisten the knot.
Last, but not least, moisten your knot with a bit of saliva. When monofilament is tightened, the friction generates enough heat to weaken the monofilament. That's why you want to wet your knot, so the next big trout you hook doesn't snap off the fly.

> "PRACTICE MAY NOT MAKE PERFECT, BUT PRACTICE DOES MAKE PROGRESS."

Gear

3 HALF-TRUTHS OF FLY RODS

Over the years, I (Steve) have learned three truths about fly rods. I stand by them and share them with new fly fishers. I also insist that these three truths are half-truths.

Each has its exceptions:

1. You get what you pay for.
My family tires of my repeating this little proverb. I say it about everything from shoes to soap to SUVs: "You get what you pay for." It's true for fly rods as well. You generally get a higher quality and performance from an $800 rod than from a $400 rod. You can also feel the difference in quality between a $150 fly rod and a $400 rod. Usually.

There are exceptions. Sometimes the feel of a rod when you cast it trumps the difference in quality. A cheaper-but-quality rod may work as well or better for you than one which costs a couple more Benjamin Franklin bills. I may be hard-pressed to tell the difference between a $350 rod and a $600 rod if I did a double-blind test.

Also, there are cases when the extra $200 gets you a particular brand name and not necessarily more quality.

2. You don't need more than one fly rod.
For trout, give me a nine-foot, six-weight rod, and I feel confident in just about any situation on the river. I've used my nine-foot, six-weight to catch selective rainbows in Nelson's Spring Creek (in Montana's Paradise Valley) on size-20 flies.

My son, Luke, even out-fished me a time or two on a small spring creek in Timber Coulee (in Wisconsin's Driftless area) with a nine-foot, six-weight while I used the more appropriate eight-foot, four weight.

Yet there are times when you need more than one fly rod. An eight-foot, four-weight might give you the only chance you have at the delicate cast required for a wary trout.

Besides, this lighter weight rod makes a 16-inch rainbow feel like a 20-inch rainbow.

> "MY FAMILY TIRES OF MY REPEATING THIS LITTLE PROVERB. I SAY IT ABOUT EVERYTHING FROM SHOES TO SOAP TO SUVS: 'YOU GET WHAT YOU PAY FOR.'"

Then there is the King salmon I hooked while fly fishing with a nine-foot, six-weight on the Willow River near Wasilla, Alaska. I thought I might defy conventional wisdom and have a chance at hauling in this monster. But I soon realized that I would break my rod if I tried to net it. I needed my eight weight to have a fighting chance.

Sure, you only need one rod. But there are times when you really do need to go a size up or down to get either distance or delicacy – not to mention the strength you need to haul in one of the big ones.

3. You don't need to worry about breakage when your rod has a generous replacement policy.

My two Orvis rods have 25-year guarantees. Orvis "will repair or replace it no matter what the reason... Step on it, close the door on it, run over it with the car – it doesn't matter, we'll fix it."

This is no lie. I've had my two rods fixed twice and replaced once. I stepped on one in the dark and broke a tip off it a couple of years later. Orvis even replaced another rod after I dropped the tip section in the Owyhee River and it drifted away!

My Winston rod has a lifetime guarantee, although it does not cover "lost rod sections, intentional breakage, misuse," etc. But when accidents happen, you don't have to kiss your $800 investment goodbye.

No need to worry, right?

Not so fast. You will be without your rod for a few weeks. Also, there is some money out of pocket. With Orvis, there is "a nominal handling charge of $30." With Winston, the handling charge jumps to $50.

And you really should take care of your fly rod even if the manufacturer has a generous replacement policy. But then again, slamming your car door on it is not the end of the world when all it takes is a few weeks and 30 bucks to get the world back to spinning happily on its axis.

"SURE, YOU ONLY NEED ONE ROD. BUT THERE ARE TIMES WHEN YOU REALLY DO NEED TO GO A SIZE UP OR DOWN TO GET EITHER DISTANCE OR DELICACY — NOT TO MENTION THE STRENGTH YOU NEED TO HAUL IN ONE OF THE BIG ONES."

Inspiration

3 HUMBLING FLY FISHING MOMENTS

Humility is not something I (Dave) necessarily seek out. But one year, I had three moments while fly fishing that put me in my place. I don't fancy myself an expert. Far from it. But I have fly fished for a lot of years. Doesn't that count for something? Apparently not.

Here are my three most humbling moments while fly fishing in a recent year:

1. Nymph fishing with a guide in Yellowstone National Park

This past year, we hired a guide for a half day. We needed some intel on the Gardner River. We didn't want to waste an entire day exploring the two- or three-mile stretch of river that we had planned to fish.

The guide (as most are) was terrific. Young. Energetic. Specific in his instructions. And dead right.

About mid morning, we hit the trail, moving from a spectacular run to another upriver. While on the trail, he said, "Let's stop and hit this little run for a few minutes." The run was against the far side of the bank and flowed towards us at a quirky angle. I had to cast my two-nymph rig from left to right, almost an over-the-shoulder toss. And to hit the hot zone required a modicum of precision.

I tried six or seven times. Nope. Couldn't make the cast. I even moved closer to the run, almost on top of the spawning browns. It wasn't more than a 15-foot cast. Not even close. The one time I hit the general vicinity of the hot zone, I couldn't get a decent dead drift to save my life.

Finally, in disgust, the guide said, "Let's just move on." I felt the sting of his non-verbal rebuke the rest of the day.

2. Mentoring a newbie fly fisher at 12,000 feet

I took a friend on a long day hike into the Colorado's Collegiate Wilderness. We hiked four miles into the lake, the last mile a lung-bursting climb.

This was his first time fly fishing. I had coached him in buying his first rod, reel, and the rest of the paraphernalia. As soon as we arrived at the high mountain lake, just several hundred yards from the Continental Divide, I began setting up his rod and reel.

I tried out his new rig first, made a cast or two, and immediately caught a rising cutthroat.

> "FINALLY, IN DISGUST, THE GUIDE SAID, 'LET'S JUST MOVE ON.' I FELT THE STING OF HIS NON-VERBAL REBUKE THE REST OF THE DAY."

I handed him the rod, made a few suggestions, and within minutes he had caught a nice cutthroat. And then another. And another.

He was one of those natural athletes. I saw no difference between how far out I was able to cast (and I had just purchased a new Sage rod!) and how far he was able to cast. At the end of the day, we caught about the same number of cutts. I was reminded that for some, fly fishing isn't all that challenging. At least not for him. On his first day. I truly felt excited for him.

I had, though, a simultaneous emotion – a touch of grumpiness. I wanted to warn him that fly fishing can only go downhill from here, that this kind of day was an aberration. But I didn't. I swallowed my sense of importance as the veteran fly fisher and cheered him on.

3. Hiking (er, sliding) down an avalanche chute
It was stupid when I was 34. And irresponsible at 54 years old.

On the way back from the high mountain lake mentioned in the previous point, I called an audible that could have been a disaster. I remembered that there was a shortcut down the mountain, an old avalanche chute now overgrown with brush and young (25-year-old) pine trees.

I had taken the shortcut 20 years earlier and forgot (or had suppressed) how steep it was.

As soon as we began to wind down the chute, sliding a few steps and then stopping, often by grabbing small trees, I felt the fear that registers deep in your soul. I snaked my way down slowly and deliberately, occasionally glancing over my shoulder to make sure my friend was making progress.

About an hour later, emotionally and physically exhausted, we arrived at the bottom of the chute. We still had another couple of hours of hiking before we reached our truck.

Nothing is more humbling than stupidity in midlife. Maybe the male brain never fully matures.

"I WAS REMINDED THAT
FOR SOME,
FLY FISHING ISN'T ALL THAT
CHALLENGING.
AT LEAST NOT FOR HIM.
ON HIS FIRST DAY.
I TRULY FELT EXCITED FOR HIM."

Tactics

3 ADJUSTMENTS WHEN FISHING STREAMERS ON SMALLER CREEKS

Fly fishing with streamers is one of the most consistent ways to catch bigger fish. Trout that gobble up bait fish and larger aquatic insects like hellgrammites get more bang for their caloric buck. More calories with less effort. A sure way to gain some heft. Pretty much how we would all love to live our lives (at least in midlife).

Recently we fished streamers on two different-sized rivers in Montana. One day we each caught 20 browns and rainbows on a smaller stream called Willow Creek, ranging from 12 to 18 inches. Two days later, we each caught one big rainbow on the Missouri River just below Hauser Dam, after four hours of slinging.

Two days of fly fishing. Two completely different rivers. Fly fishing streamers in smaller trout streams is simply different than slinging a rig in larger waters like the Missouri. Here are three adjustments that fly fishers need to make when fly fishing with streamers on smaller creeks:

1. Casting Downstream

For starters, you tend to get only one or two shots at the pocket of water in a smaller stream, so your cast needs to be precise. Most likely you're not going to rip out four or five fish from one small run.

On Willow Creek, with the stream as low as it was that year, more often than not we got above the run, cast downstream, and then made three or four strips. Sometimes, we crawled to the bank near the middle of the run and then cast downstream and then stripped back the streamer.

On the Mighty Mo (Missouri), we cast as far as we could sling the streamer, slightly upstream, with a nine foot, eight weight fly rod. We mended the line once after the cast and then let the streamer drift until it began to swing. Then we stripped back the line. There were three of us fly fishing, and we cycled through about a 200-yard stretch of river.

Big river, big open spaces, big casts.

> "YOU TEND TO GET ONLY ONE OR TWO SHOTS AT THE POCKET OF WATER IN A SMALLER STREAM, SO YOUR CAST NEEDS TO BE PRECISE."

2. Quicker Retrieves

In the smaller creek, of course, there isn't a lot of time to retrieve the line. Casts are shorter, and the distance from the end of the swing back to your fly rod is short. Sometimes, shorter one- to three-inch strips seem to work best. Other times, six-inch strips seem to work.

In tight spaces, you may get only three or four strips, and then it's time to cast again. On the Missouri, stripping the line was less frenetic. We had lots of time to retrieve the streamer. There's a rule of thumb that goes something like this: If you're fishing slower water, then make your strips faster, and if the river is faster, make your strips slower.

The more precise rule of thumb is: Try several ways to retrieve your line, and go with one that works.

3. Weight Forward Line

In smaller streams, we never use sink tip line. The runs are likely not that deep, maybe mid-thigh or waist-deep at most. However, on bigger rivers (and beaver ponds), fly fishers may need sink tip line to get the streamer down fast enough and deep enough.

It's okay to use a weight forward line on smaller creeks, but on the larger rivers, its essential to have a spare reel with sink tip line in your truck.

"THERE'S A RULE OF THUMB THAT GOES SOMETHING LIKE THIS: IF YOU'RE FISHING SLOWER WATER, THEN MAKE YOUR STRIPS FASTER, AND IF THE RIVER IS FASTER, MAKE YOUR STRIPS SLOWER."

Safety

4 BENEFITS OF A FLY FISHING BUDDY

I (Steve) enjoy solitude when I fly fish. Yet I rarely fly fish alone. I like to fly fish with a buddy, if only because there's someone to take pics of my big fish. The truth is, it is better to fly fish with a buddy or a brother or a sister or a spouse. Why is a fishing partner such a big deal? Here are four benefits of fly fishing with a buddy or someone else:

1. Safety

This is at the top of the list for a reason. Your life may depend on it.

Recently, I slipped at the edge of a small stream I was fishing and fell forward in some shallow water. The only casualty was a cracked fly box. But I reflected later on how I could have hit my head on a nearby boulder and passed out. If I had been alone, that could have been disastrous, even in shallow water. I was glad that my podcast partner, Dave, was only 30 yards away.

Since I wasn't hurt, he got a good laugh. But had I been hurt, he was there to help.

We also regularly fish in grizzly bear country, so having two fly fishers — each armed with bear spray — is critical.

> "I STARTED SETTING THE HOOK EVERY TIME MY STRIKE INDICATOR MADE A SLIGHT BUMP. EVERY TIME, TAKING DAVE'S SUGGESTION RESULTED IN HOOKING A FISH."

2, Problem-Solving

Another benefit of fly fishing with a buddy is having another brain.

Recently, Dave and I were fishing for fall browns in the Gardner River in Yellowstone National Park. We took turns drifting our nymphs through the same run. We were catching fish, but Dave pointed out to me that I was missing some strikes. He suggested that the almost imperceptible hesitation of my strike indicator was a subtle strike. So I started setting the hook every time my strike indicator made a slight bump. Every time, taking Dave's suggestion resulted in hooking a fish.

3. Sharing the Joy

There's something satisfying about sharing the moment with someone else. When Dave and I catch fish, we whoop it up together. I can honestly say I enjoy watching Dave catch big trout (okay, as long as I'm catching them too!). Like any other joy in life, fly fishing is meant to be shared. This goes beyond catching trout, though. It extends to seeing the sun flood a beautiful meadow, watching a couple of wolves saunter along the bank of the Yellowstone River, or hearing the piercing bugle of a bull elk on a September morning.

4. Remembering

As much as I try to slow down in the moment and take in the experience, I find that I forget certain aspects of a day on the river. That's why I force myself to share dinner at the end of the day with my fly fishing buddies. Well, okay, I really don't have to force myself to do this! Dinner is the capstone of a great day. Often, the dinner conversation I have with Dave or my brother or one of my sons will remind me of moments or experiences I had forgotten.

Sometimes, even years later, I'll be talking about a certain trip with one of them, and they will remind me of some moment or experience that had vanished from my memory.

As a wise writer once said, "Two is better than one... if either of them falls down, one can help the other up... Though they may be overpowered, two can defend themselves" (Eccl. 4:9-10, 12). While that applies to all of life, it certainly relates directly to your next fly fishing adventure.

"LIKE ANY OTHER JOY IN LIFE,
FLY FISHING
IS MEANT
TO BE SHARED.
THIS GOES BEYOND
CATCHING TROUT, THOUGH.
IT EXTENDS TO SEEING
THE SUN FLOOD
A BEAUTIFUL MEADOW,
WATCHING A COUPLE OF WOLVES
SAUNTER ALONG THE BANK
OF THE YELLOWSTONE RIVER,
OR HEARING
THE PIERCING BUGLE
OF A BULL ELK ON A
SEPTEMBER MORNING."

Gear

5 REASONS YOU NEED A WADING STAFF

A year ago, I (Steve) bought a wading staff for use on the big rivers of the American West — particularly the Yellowstone and the Missouri. I had visions of strapping it to my side only for use in thigh-deep or even waist-deep water. But I also discovered that it's worth wearing on small streams when I'm only wading in ankle-deep water. Dave and I were getting ready to fish Willow Creek south of Three Forks, Montana, with a good friend. I was mildly surprised to see our friend strap on his collapsible wading staff. But when he explained to me why he always wears it, I decided to take mine out of my duffel bag and give it a try.

Now I'm a believer. Here are the reasons why it makes sense to use a wading staff even when you're on a small stream in shallow water:

1. Traction

This is one of the two reasons my friend cited. Even with state-of-the-art wading boots, moss-covered rocks can be slick. I was pleased how my wading staff helped me stay upright when one of my boots slipped.

2. Stability

I'm in reasonably good shape at midlife. But my legs are not as strong as they were when I was in my late thirties and early forties. I found that a "third leg" gave me more stability when I walked on the rock banks, as well as the boulders in shallow water.

3. Stamina

I was also surprised how my "third leg" took pressure off my two legs. We fished three miles up Willow Creek in a canyon which lacked any trails or gentle banks. Then we walked three miles down in and along the creek. My legs were not nearly as tired as I expected after the six-mile trek.

4. Snakes

This is the second reason my friend always carries his wading staff. We were in rattlesnake country, and even though it was mid-October,

> "I FOUND THAT A 'THIRD LEG' GAVE ME MORE STABILITY WHEN I WALKED ON THE ROCK BANKS, AS WELL AS THE BOULDERS IN SHALLOW WATER."

some fishing buddies of his encountered a rattler a few days before on the stretch of creek we were fishing. I'm no advocate of killing snakes. But I like the idea of packing something that can ward off a rattler when a surprise encounter happens.

5. Climbing

I've also found that my wading staff makes it easier to scramble up steep banks and rocky inclines. Now I understand why another friend raved about the walking staff he carried in the Swiss Alps.

> "I'VE ALSO FOUND THAT MY WADING STAFF MAKES IT EASIER TO SCRAMBLE UP STEEP BANKS AND ROCKY INCLINES. NOW I UNDERSTAND WHY ANOTHER FRIEND RAVED ABOUT THE WALKING STAFF HE CARRIED IN THE SWISS ALPS."

There are affordable alternatives, if you don't want to purchase a fly fishing wading staff; some fly fishers use an old ski pole or even a mountaineer's staff or simply find a thick branch along the river.

But if you're in the market for a wading staff, check out the ones made by Simms and Orvis. I tried them both, and I give the nod to the Orvis model because it snaps into place almost instantly. Both of these staffs are collapsible, although I generally keep mine assembled most of the day.

In the Old Testament, when King David composed the 23rd psalm, he was not referring to a fly rod nor a wading staff when he wrote, "Thy rod and thy staff, they comfort me." But still, I find comfort in taking both a rod and staff with me – even when I walk through quiet waters.

Tactics

7 TIPS FOR BETTER FLY FISHING PHOTOS

The only things you want to leave behind when you fly fish are the trout you caught. The only things you want to take with you are photos. With social media, particularly Instagram and its filters, any photo can be touched up, altered, and manipulated.

If you follow fly fishing guides, outfitters, or other fly fishers on Instagram, you know the deep colors and tints and shadows used to re-do photos. In addition to Instagram's filters, the photo filter apps are legion. But engaging photos begin with, well, taking a great photo. Filters can only do so much. Most fly fishers will opt for a cell phone camera rather than, say, a Nikon single-lens-reflex camera with a zoom lens. Today's phones take great photos, if you pay attention to these seven basic tips:

1. **Keep the sun out of the background.**
If the sun is behind the fly fisher you intend to photograph, your

camera lens will do the same thing your eye does when it looks into the sun. It will squint. This allows less light into the picture, making it dark. So keep the sun beside you or behind you. If you're taking a photo at high noon, this will not be an issue.

Similarly, if your subject is in the shade, make sure that the background is not lit up by the sun. Shade can be your friend because it lessens the shadows that hide your subject's face. But a sunlit patch behind the shade will turn your photo dark.

2. Put a red hat or bandana on your fly fisher.

A red hat or bandana or shirt might spook a trout. But it sure adds a lot to your photo! Red provides a vivid, pleasing contrast to all the earth tones – the greens, browns, and blues.

> "A RED HAT OR BANDANA OR SHIRT MIGHT SPOOK A TROUT. BUT IT SURE ADDS A LOT TO YOUR PHOTO!"

3. Get some close up shots.

Skilled photographers move in close. If you're photographing a fish, fill the frame. Similarly, zoom in on your fly fisher friend. Or take a couple of steps closer. Yes, there is a place for a shot in the distance. But close-up shots are more interesting and generally exude more life.

4. Photograph scenery in the early morning and early evening.

Look at the scenery shots on your favorite calendar or book cover. The reason for the vivid colors is not the $2000 lens (although that does not hurt). It's all about time of day. The light in the early morning and early evening brings scenery to life. The shadows add a striking contrast that flattens out during mid-day.

5. Include an object in the foreground.
This gives depth to your photos and can even provide a kind of frame that accents them. A tree branch or a bush or a rock in the foreground can do wonders for the picture you are trying to compose. You can also use the bottom half of your fly rod with the reel.

> "A TREE BRANCH OR A BUSH OR A ROCK IN THE FOREGROUND CAN DO WONDERS FOR THE PICTURE YOU ARE TRYING TO COMPOSE."

6. Think in thirds.
If you're photographing a stretch of river with the sky in the background, it's easy to get the horizontal dividing line (between land and sky) in the middle of the photo. This breaks the photo into equal halves — an upper and lower section. Don't do this. It results in a bland photo.

Instead, devote either the top third or the top two-thirds to the sky. This disproportion makes your photo more arresting.
Also, when you include a fly fisher in a landscape-shaped photo, keep them out of the middle. Again, this is boring. The photography

police may issue a warrant for your arrest. Instead, imagine that your landscape-shaped photo has been divided into three vertical panels. Put the fly fisher in either the panel to the left or the panel to the right. If your fly fisher is facing left, place her in the right panel. If your fly fisher is facing right, place him in the left panel. Why, you say? Take a photo which breaks this rule and you'll see how silly it looks.

> "DEVOTE EITHER THE TOP THIRD OR THE TOP TWO-THIRDS TO THE SKY. THIS DISPROPORTION MAKES YOUR PHOTO MORE ARRESTING."

7. Keep your camera (cell phone) in a zip-lock bag.

You can't take photos if your cell phone or camera is water-logged. So make sure you have some zip-lock bags. You never know when you'll drop your phone into the river. Or you might slip and soak the section of your fly vest with the pouch containing your phone.

Inspiration

10 WAYS TO COPE WITH THE FLY FISHING OFF SEASON

How does a fly fisher who doesn't live minutes from great fly fishing water cope in the winter off season? We've come up with a few coping strategies, since we both live in the 'burbs of Chicago:

1. Go through the photos of your last trip.
Thumb through the photos on your cell phone. This brings back good memories and helps you relive the best moments. Warning: Your photos might result in you laughing out loud or shouting "Yes!"

2. Make a list of the year's best memories.
After you've thumbed through your photos, write down your favorite memories from the last year of fly fishing. Making a list will preserve your memories and maybe even remind you of a detail you had forgotten.

3. Take inventory of your gear.
This is an act of hope. It's a reminder that you will fly fish again. Besides, it really does prepare you for your next trip.

4. Shop for something new.
This is the benefit – or liability – of the previous strategy. When you take inventory of your gear, you may discover your need for a new reel, new gloves, a new fly box, or a new net. This sends you on a mission to research options and prices. It keeps your mind off the reality that you are not able to fish.

> "AFTER YOU'VE THUMBED THROUGH YOUR PHOTOS, WRITE DOWN YOUR FAVORITE MEMORIES FROM THE LAST YEAR OF FLY FISHING."

5. Visit the trout at your local Bass Pro Shop.
A couple of times during the winter, Steve visits his local Bass Pro Shop and stands on a little bridge and looks wistfully at the 20-inch rainbows that swim in the little creek on the edge of the aisle with coffee mugs and pocket knives.

Seriously! He is trying to muster the courage to ask the store manager if he can fly fish the stream since he is a catch-and-release fly fisher. Seeing him catch these rainbows might get more people interested in fly fishing, and then they would spend more money at Bass Pro.

It's a win-win, right?

6. Watch fly fishing videos.
The internet is loaded with videos of fly fishers catching trout.

Start with websites like Orvis or Winston. Then, go to YouTube and search for just about any river or species of trout that piques your interest.

7. Tie a few flies.
This only works if you are a fly tyer. If you're not, the off-season is a good time to take your first class.

8. Read a good fly fishing book.
Read about the areas you want to fly fish. For example, if you're headed to Montana or Wyoming, get a copy of *Bud Lilly's Guide to Fly Fishing the New West*. It's an entertaining read with humor and history woven into it.

Read for skill development. Gary Borger's "Fly Fishing" series is ideal for this. His fourth book in the series, *The Angler as Predator*, has helped us a lot.

You might even educate yourself on the flies you're trying to imitate with a book like *Pocketguide to Western Hatches* by Dave Hughes or *Matching Major Eastern Hatches: New Patterns for Selective Trout* by Henry Ramsay.

Don't forget to read through the lists you compiled from previous years (see #2 above).

9. Plan your next trip.
There's nothing like planning your next trip to get the juices flowing! The off-season is a great time to do some research on new places, or to plan for a visit to some good old places.

10. Watch the movie "A River Runs Through It."
You owe it to yourself to watch this at least once a year. The cinema-

tography alone makes it worthwhile. The story is gripping, too. Real men might even shed a tear or two at the last scene.

Alright, something in the above list is guaranteed to help you cope with the fly fishing off-season. If not, watch college football and college basketball. Go hunting. Remodel your kitchen.

Oh yes, you might even consider a few hours on the water in the dead of winter if you're within a day's drive of a river or stream. Whatever you do to pass the time, winter will soon lift and the rivers will come to life in the spring.

> "THE OFF-SEASON IS A GREAT TIME TO DO SOME RESEARCH ON NEW PLACES, OR TO PLAN FOR A VISIT TO SOME GOOD OLD PLACES."

Safety

7 STRATEGIES TO FLY FISH IN WINTER WITHOUT LOSING IT

Winter is not our favorite season to fly fish. But there is a mystique to fishing the big rivers of Montana or the spring creeks in Minnesota a few days before Christmas or a couple of weeks into the new year. If you fly fish in winter, be careful to do so without losing it. We're using the pronoun "it" to refer to everything from your sanity, to the feeling in your fingers, to life itself. The frustration and the dangers intensify in the winter.

Here are seven strategies for keeping your sanity and your life intact:

1. Lower your expectations.
Don't expect a 20-fish day. Trout feed, but not as aggressively as they will when winter gives way to spring. Don't expect that your hands will stay warm. Don't expect the guides on your fly rod to remain ice-free.

2. Wait for mid-day and early afternoon.
Trout respond better in these brief periods of warmth. You may, too. So sleep in and quit early. While we're on the topic of warmth, wait for a warmer day. Tie flies or read a fly fishing book when weather is in the teens.

3. Focus on shallow water, not deep pools.
Bud Lilly, one of the deans of western fly fishing, assumed the fish in deep pools were not feeding as actively as fish in shallow riffles. Deep pools do not get enough sunlight, while the sun can trigger insect activity or even the metabolism of a sluggish trout in a shallow riffle.

4. Try nymphs first.
We've had some decent midge fishing in January on Montana's Madison River. But unless you get into rising fish, nymphs may be your best bet. Trout do not seem to chase streamers as aggressively (if they chase them at all) as they will when the water temperatures get warmer.

5. Avoid wading in deep water.
Slipping and falling into the river on a 30-degree day is much different than on an 80-degree day in July. In July, a bath might cost you your dignity. In January, it might cost you your life.

> "TROUT RESPOND BETTER IN BRIEF PERIODS OF WARMTH. YOU MAY, TOO. SO SLEEP IN AND QUIT EARLY."

6. Go with a buddy.
This is always the safest approach to fly fishing, but it's even more critical in the winter. A sprained knee a quarter mile from your vehicle could be a disaster in cold temperatures if you are alone.

7. Dress for warmth.
It goes without saying, but pile on those layers. Put on waterproof gloves. Cover your face with a neck gator or a face mask. Double up on socks, too. Wear a wool or fur or polyester fleece hat. The folks at Harvard Medical School say that without a hat you can lose up to 50 percent of your body heat in certain cold-weather conditions even if the rest of your body is bundled up.

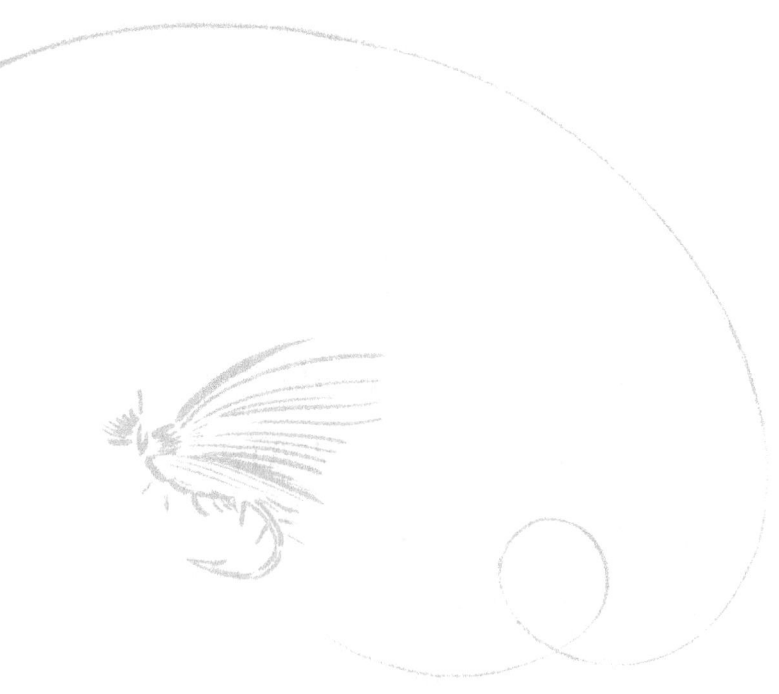

FINAL THOUGHT:

THE JURY IS OUT ON WHETHER YOU WANT CLOUDS OR SUN FOR WINTER FLY FISHING. A FRIEND AND VETERAN FLY FISHER IN MONTANA USED TO SAY, "THE WORST DAY FOR FLY FISHING IS A SUNNY DAY IN FEBRUARY." OUR EXPERIENCE SUGGESTS HE IS RIGHT. YET, AS NOTED EARLIER, BUD LILLY OBSERVED THAT SUNLIGHT CAN TRIGGER CERTAIN INSECT HATCHES, PARTICULARLY THE BIG "SNOWFLIES" THAT APPEAR ON MANY BIG RIVERS BEGINNING IN FEBRUARY.

Tactics

5 PROBLEMS WITH YOUR CAST AND HOW TO FIX THEM

Here are five common casting struggles of fly fishers and a couple of solutions for each one:

1. Your casts lack distance.
There are two quick fixes if your casts come up short of your target.

First, flick your wrist. Practice this before you pick up your fly rod. Make a handgun out of your casting hand (index finger extended, thumb up, bottom three fingers pointing back at you). Now snap forward, then back, then forward, then back. That's the action you want when casting your rod.

Too many fly fishers try to be graceful and end up waving their arms forward and backward. But a graceful cast is the product of snapping the wrists (like a baseball pitcher throwing the curve that troubles hitters). The second quick fix is to make sure that your rod is parallel with the ground on your final forward cast.

Many fly fishers keep their rods pointing up at a 45° angle as their line shoots towards its target. But as legendary fly fisher Gary Borger observes, this creates "all sorts of shoot-shortening friction." He even suggests lifting the rod butt as a way of keeping your rod parallel to the surface of the ground (or water).

2. Your casts lack accuracy.

Here are two solutions to inaccurate casting. They seem too simple to be true.

First, keep your eyes on the target. Yes, some folks have better hand-eye coordination than others. But it is remarkable how this simple tip enhances accuracy.

Second, point your tip at the target. It seems silly to make such an obvious point. As soon as you make a conscious effort to point the eye of your rod tip towards the spot where you want the fly to land (even as your rod is parallel to the ground as discussed in #1 above), your accuracy will improve.

3. Your casts result in tangled line.

Once again, here are two adjustments you can make. First, stop false casting so much. The more you false cast, the more opportunity you give your line to tangle.

> "KEEP YOUR EYES ON THE TARGET... IT IS REMARKABLE HOW THIS SIMPLE TIP ENHANCES ACCURACY."

Second, make sure you allow your backcast to unfurl. A lot of tangles happen because fly fishers hurry from backcast to forward cast. This is a recipe for either snapping off the fly (the bullwhip effect) or for tangling line that has not had time to unfurl.

4. Your casts spook the fish.
One problem is that the shadow of your fly line spooks the fish. This is an easy fix. Stop false casting so much! That's all. If the problem is that you're slapping the line on the water, then there is a simple trick to help your line land softly.

The trick is to pull your rod tip up at the last moment. Ideally, your rod tip is pointed at your target (#2) and your rod is parallel to the ground (#3). At the last moment, make a slight upward pull on your rod. I like to think of it as a gentle hiccup. What this does is to stop the forward momentum of the line. It goes limp and falls gently to the surface of the water. This takes some practice, but it really does work.

> "MAKE SURE YOU ALLOW YOUR BACKCAST TO UNFURL. A LOT OF TANGLES HAPPEN BECAUSE FLY FISHERS HURRY FROM BACKCAST TO FORWARD CAST."

5. Your casts get wrecked by the wind.

Here is a sure-fire solution for this problem: Quit. Yes, just quit. Call it a day. Head for the truck and drive to your favorite restaurant. But there are some other alternatives to quitting for the day:

First, stop false casting. Yes, that's a solution to a lot of problems, including wind.

Second, move in closer and shorten up your casts. If the wind is howling enough to make casting difficult, it's also creating ripples on the surface which will keep trout from seeing your movements.

Third, a guide once said to make a strong backcast and a softer forward cast. That's the opposite of our instincts, so it takes some practice. But it really does work.

Tactics

9 FLY FISHING MOMENTS THAT REQUIRE DIFFERENT SPEEDS

Movies tend to romanticize the fly fishing experience. The natural beauty, the sound of the rushing river, and the rhythmic motion of the cast — all conspire to create an image of tranquility. The entire experience appears to be one speed: slow motion. The reality, though, is that there are at least three speeds to fly fishing: go, slow, and stop. In the spirit of the stoplight, green means go, yellow means slow, and red means stop! Here are nine fly fishing moments that require different speeds:

1. Before you step into the river to fly fish — RED.
As you approach the river, stop a few yards before the river's edge. Observe.

Even if you're wading into the river at a public access area, don't simply traipse into the water and move upstream (or downstream). Wait a few minutes. Do you see any fish rising? Is the stream or river lower?

Higher? Do you see any insects in the air or on the water? Start your fly fishing with a modicum of observation.

2. After you fish for 15 minutes – GREEN.
Beginner fly fishers tend to find a decent run and cast in the same spot for hours. Unless you are working a steelhead run in a larger river, most likely you need to move to the next run more quickly than you are.

After 10 to 15 minutes, move to the next run. Truly. Don't keep flailing the pool or run. Just move on. If there is another fly fisher in the run in front of you, go around him or her – perhaps to a stretch of river that is several runs ahead of him or her. There are exceptions to every rule, but in general, green means go when you are fly fishing in smaller streams and rivers.

> "THERE ARE AT LEAST THREE SPEEDS TO FLY FISHING: GO, SLOW, AND STOP. IN THE SPIRIT OF THE STOPLIGHT, GREEN MEANS GO, YELLOW MEANS SLOW, AND RED MEANS STOP!"

3. Approaching your next run – YELLOW.
This is a corollary to #1 and #2. Most stretches of rivers do not have unlimited runs – ergo, places where the trout lie. Treat each run like the treasure that it is. Don't just step into the river and begin slinging.

Slow down to look for rising trout. Check to see if you are casting a shadow over the run you're trying to fish. Don't waste the opportunity that is in front of you. Be methodical as you fish. Act as if every run is the last run of the day.

4. Tying knots – YELLOW.
It's tempting to cave in to your excitement (or anxiety) to get back to fly fishing after you have snapped off your fly. Don't. Slow down and tie a good knot. Make sure you haven't weakened the monofilament when you tightened the knot.

5. Reeling in fish – GREEN and YELLOW.
This requires two speeds. The goal is always to release the fish as fast as you can. The time you hook the fish to the time you release it is crucial to its survival. Never should you "play" the fish. It's green all the way.

However, if you hook a large fish, you will suddenly realize the impossibility of simply cranking in the fish. You'll need to slow down to work your drag, pull the fish from side to side to wear it out, and move downstream to a shallow part of the river to net it.

If you want to catch a large brown trout on your three-pound tippet, you'll need to slow down. Really slow down.

6. Wading – YELLOW.
Nothing good comes from trying to move through the river quickly, even in slower moving streams. Speed increases your risk of falling. Slow down to enjoy the experience and to preserve your life.

7. After you see lightning or hear thunder — RED and GREEN.
This is patently obvious, but you'll want to stop ("red") fly fishing and run ("green") to find a low spot (not under a tree!). Make sure you leave your fly rod on the ground in a safe place but a good many yards away from you. Or your Winston rod may become a lightning rod!

8. When you encounter a bison or moose or grizzly — RED.
It's never a good idea to saunter up to any wild animal or even to run away from a startling encounter. Stop. Maybe even curl up into the fetal position if the wild encounter is a grizzly bear. Hopefully, you have a canister of bear spray around your waist.

9. After a great day on the river — GREEN.
Green means go to the nearest supper club or rib and chop house. Go with a cold beverage, and go with the largest rib-eye on the menu.

"ACT AS IF EVERY RUN IS THE LAST RUN OF THE DAY."

Waters

5 UNLIKELY PLACES TO CATCH TROUT

You might be surprised at some of the unlikely places where you can catch trout on your fly rod. Here are five places you might not want to overlook:

1. In town
Steve once landed a 12-pound salmon on a Woolly Bugger within the city limits of Milwaukee, Wisconsin, about nine minutes north of the Bradley Center where the Milwaukee Bucks play basketball.

Don't ignore the city limits if a river runs through it.

2. In shallow water
This will come as no surprise to veteran fly fishers. Trout will make their way into shallow waters to sip flies.

Pay attention to what is going on in shallow water before you neglect it or wade through it.

3. Near a fishing access
It may seem like a waste of time to fish within a hundred yards or so

of a fishing access because everybody else does. But the truth is, they don't. They assume everyone else has fished these spots. So no one does.

4. Where someone else has just fished
We both like to fish untouched water. If someone else has fished a run a few minutes before, we're tempted to skip it. But a few runs are so good that they are worth fishing shortly after the previous fly fisher leaves them.

Even if you're not as skilled as the fly fisher who preceded you, the different look you provide might turn out to be the right magic. Perhaps the fly pattern you use or the different depth at which you fish will coax a trout to take your offering.

Keep in mind that your chances increase with the size of the river. If someone else has fished a run on a small stream, the trout will generally need more time to get back into their feeding patterns. The disturbance factor is simply greater than in a run on a large river.

5. In the grass
Yes, this works – but only if we're talking about a side channel that runs through the grass. Admittedly, this venue can be frustrating. These channels are narrow, and the blades of grass that flank them love to grab your fly if you don't get it exactly in the center of the channel.

We've caught some big brook trout, though, in these grass channels in meadows where rivers flow. Beaver dams often create this phenomenon, but so does high water.

Keep your options open.

We're not ready to abandon the wild places. But there is a thrill of catching a trout in an irrigation ditch or in a run right along the highway.

Education

INTERPRETING THE 4 FEEDING BEHAVIORS OF TROUT

While it is not an exact science, you can generally figure out what trout are feeding on by watching their behavior. The key word is "generally":

1. Noses mean duns.
The dun stage is the first of two adult stages of mayflies. If you see noses poking through the surface, the trout are feeding on mayflies in their dun stage. Sometimes, these trout appear to be standing on their fins, up to their eyeballs in water.

A Parachute Adams may work fine. But in some cases – slow, clear water or a specific hatch – it might pay to use a Comparadun or Sparkle Dun pattern.

Some kind of cripple pattern may work, too, given that most aquatic insects do not make the transition from nymph to adult stage and remain stuck in the surface film.

2. Fins mean nymphs.

If you see only a dorsal fin or tail (and not the trout's nose), then the trout is feeding on something just below the surface. This may be a good time to use an unweighted nymph, which floats just beneath the surface. Or, you can use an emerger pattern which sits low and protrudes into the film beneath it.

A pattern which rides high, like a Parachute Adams, will not work well unless it gets water-logged and disappears from your sight.

3. Dimples mean midges or spinners.

If you see a small dimple in the water, chances are the trout are feeding on midges or spent mayfly spinners. You may or may not see the trout's nose. Sometimes you will even see the trout gently roll through the surface with the grace of a dolphin.

Aside from specific midge patterns, a size #20 Parachute Adams works well for midges.

Mayfly spinner patterns have light bodies and wings which lay out to the side (like airplane wings) rather than shooting up from the body at a $45°$ angle.

4. Splashes mean caddis.

If you see rising trout making splashes, they are likely feeding on caddis flies. The reason for the splash is that these flies are fluttering on the surface, and the trout go into attack mode. Some kind of Elk Hair Caddis pattern will do the trick.

As always, talk to the experts at your local fly shop or read their reports online. Then keep your eyes open to watch what is happening on the river's surface.

"RISING TROUT MAKING SPLASHES ARE LIKELY FEEDING ON CADDIS FLIES."

Flies

7 BASIC FACTS ABOUT MAYFLIES

We don't always think about mayflies, but when we do, we usually catch more trout. Here are seven facts you need to know about *Ephemeroptera* — the insect order that's popularly known as mayflies.

We've learned these seven key insights from our mentors, guides we've used, and from the writings of Dave Hughes and Jim Schollmeyer:

1. All but one or two days of a mayfly's 365-day life span is spent underwater.
This is the nymph stage. No wonder 85% of a trout's diet comes from beneath the surface. It's why fishing nymphs is almost always a sure bet.

2. Most mayflies hatch at mid-day.
This means that 11 a.m. to 2 p.m. is prime time — depending, of course, on wind and water temperature. Overcast, cool days are ideal, especially for Baetis flies and Blue-Winged Olives (BWOs).

3. Mayfly duns ride the surface until their upright wings are dry and hardened for flight.

The ride through the current typically lasts for 10 to 20 feet. Obviously, this makes the duns vulnerable to rising trout. And these rising trout are vulnerable to your mayfly imitation.

4. If rising trout ignore the mayfly duns on the surface, they are feeding on emergers.

The emerger stage is the brief transition between the nymph stage and the dun stage. The child becomes an adult when the skin splits along the back of the nymph and the winged dun escapes. Wise anglers will put on an emerger pattern in these moments.

5. Once duns turn into spinners, they mate in the air and the females deposit their eggs.

At this point, the females are spent and fall to the water. This creates a "spinner fall" — another opportunity for a trout feeding frenzy.

Anglers who see mayflies with flat wings like an airplane rather than with wings sticking up should switch to a spinner pattern.

6. Mayflies vary in size and in the time of year they appear.

In the western rivers, BWOs generally hatch from mid-March through May. Pale Morning Duns (PMDs) are more prominent from May through August. Then BWOs show up in force again in September.

Typical sizes range from 14 through 18. But the brown and green Drakes in Henry's Fork of the Snake River, for example, are larger — from size 10 to 12.

7. Mayflies need cold, clean water.

Water pollution makes mayflies disappear. When mayflies disappear, the trout do too. So water conservation is vital to trout fishing.

Inspiration

4 "MORE" FLY FISHING MYTHS

There's a four-letter word fly fishers should use with caution.

It's not the word you mutter or yell when your backcast catches your fly on a pine branch. Rather, it's a word that can mislead you. It can also set you up for disappointment. The four-letter word is ... "more." Here are four fly-fishing myths involving the word "more":

1. The more I fly fish, the better I will become.
Practice does not make perfect. Practice makes permanent.

So instead of repeating bad habits, concentrate on improving your cast or your knowledge of insect hatches. Watch an instructional video. Read a book. Hire a guide for a day. The more you work on the craft of fly fishing, the better you will become.

2. I will fly fish more if I move to a prime fly fishing area.
Steve lived in Montana for two decades near several blue-ribbon trout waters. Yet he found that life often got in the way of fly fishing. The

truth is, most folks have to work for a living, and the grind of living eats away at your time on the river.

So don't despair if you have to travel a long way to find good fly fishing. You can accomplish a lot more in a three-day fly fishing trip than you think. If you do live in a prime fly fishing area, figure out how to overcome the obstacles that keep you from the river.

3. I will fly fish more at the next stage of my life.
Good luck with that!

Busy college years give way to busy work years. Having a family and settling down means endless school plays, football games, volleyball matches, and band concerts. By the way, we loved every minute of this stage in our lives! But it does eat up fly fishing time.

> "SO DON'T DESPAIR IF YOU HAVE TO TRAVEL A LONG WAYS TO FIND GOOD FLY FISHING. YOU CAN ACCOMPLISH A LOT MORE IN A THREE-DAY FLY FISHING TRIP THAN YOU THINK."

At least there is retirement, right? Perhaps. But the stage of life that affords more time diminishes your energy. That older body can't take quite as much. So don't wait for life to slow down.

Get out there now. Tomorrow will have scheduling issues of its own.

4. The more fish I catch, the more satisfied I will be.
We both love catching a lot of trout. But sometimes, it's hard to slow down the moment and savor it when you catch a trout on every cast.

Not that we're complaining about those magic moments when we do!

Also, there is no magic number at which we are sated. After catching fish number 32, we're just as greedy to catch our 33rd. Strangely enough, we've had three-fish days that are as satisfying as 40-fish days because we've had to overcome some challenges to catch them. We've learned to savor each fish we catch, to slow down the moment rather than rushing to catch "one more."

We're tempted to add a few more lists to our book. But we'll end it here. Life is short. You need to put the book down and get out on the river. We sure hope our lists will help you get more enjoyment out of fly fishing.

And catch more fish.

Tag Index

EDUCATION

The 3 Biological Drives of Trout 6
5 Ways to Be a Conservationist 14
7 Ways to Make the Most of Public Access 34
4 Ways to Encourage Your Kids to Fly Fish 48
Interpreting the 4 Feeding Behaviors of Trout 156

FLIES

6 Common Dry Fly Attractor Patterns 8
5 Reasons I (Steve) Took Up Fly Tying 24
6 Reasons I (Dave) Don't Tie Flies 26
Dave's 5 Favorite Nymph and Wet Fly Patterns 54
Steve's 5 Favorite Nymph and Wet Fly Patterns 56
4 Reminders Before You Fish a Hatch 84
8 Tips to Start "Mousing" 94
7 Basic Facts About Mayflies 158

GEAR

4 Questions before Buying Your First Fly Rod 52
5 Questions before You Buy Your Next Pair of Waders 58
9 Items to Weather the Weather 90

164

5 Questions before You Set Up Your New Reel 104
3 Half-Truths of Fly Rods 114
5 Reasons You Need a Wading Staff 130

INSPIRATION

Bob's 8 Pearls of Fly Fishing Wisdom 2
5 Traits of the Successful Fly Fisher 4
3 Fly Fishing Lessons From My Father 18
3 Reasons Why I (Steve) Fly Fish 40
8 Fly Fishing Personalities 46
6 Elements of a Satisfying Day on the River 60
5 Disciplines to Fly Fish More 74
3 Takeaways from "A River Runs Through It" 78
8 Stupid Things We've Done While Fly Fishing 88
Our 6 Favorite Outdoor Authors 96
3 Humbling Fly Fishing Moments 118
10 Ways to Cope with the Fly Fishing Off Season 138
4 "More" Fly Fishing Myths 160

SAFETY

10 Commandments of Wading 16
8 Additional Safe Wading Tips 30
7 Fly Fishing Safety Devices 44

Tag Index

7 More Safe Wading Tips 62
5 Wild Animals to Observe at a Distance 64
5 Precautions to Take While Fly Fishing 66
5 Common Fly Fishing Dangers 72
8 Smart Reactions When You Fall into the River 106
4 Benefits of a Fly Fishing Buddy 126
7 Strategies to Fly Fish in Winter Without Losing It 142

TACTICS

11 Reasons You're Not Catching Trout 10
Nymph Fishing's 7 Nagging Questions 20
3 Disciplines to Master Spring Creek Fly Fishing 28
5 Quick Tips to Catching More Trout on Hoppers 36
3 Truths about the Mother's Day Caddis Hatch 50
12 Simple Fly Fishing Hacks 68
4 Practices to Break Out of a Fly Fishing Slump 70
4 Ways to Make Fly Fishing Simple 76
8 Adjustments to Make for Spring Creeks 100
5 Truths When Fishing Dry Flies After Dark 108
7 Spots to Cast Your Dry Fly 110
4 Notes on Fly Fishing Knots 112
3 Adjustments When Fishing Streamers on Smaller Creeks 122
7 Tips for Better Fly Fishing Photos 134
5 Problems with Your Cast and How to Fix Them 146
9 Fly Fishing Moments that Require Different Speeds ... 150

TRIPS

6 Ways to Spoil Your Guided Trip	12
6 Planning Tips for Your Fly Fishing Trip	38
10 Reasons to Fish the Yellowstone Ecosystem	42
5 Tips When Fishing the Yellowstone Ecosystem	80
5 Lessons from a Recent Fly Fishing Trip	86
3 Ways to Track Your Adventures	92
Our 6 Favorite Eateries in the Yellowstone Ecosystem	102

WATERS

5 Tips for Fly Fishing Lakes	22
The 3 Kinds of Rivers You'll Fly Fish	98
5 Unlikely Places to Catch Trout	154

About the fly fishers

DAVE GOETZ

1. Dave has a wife, four kids, and a Golden Retriever.
Dave is the same age as Steve, but Dave and Jana got married almost 10 years after Steve and Pris. So Dave and Jana's kids are a lot younger (about 10 years younger) than Steve and Pris'.

2. Dave is a marketing guy.
Dave is the founder of CZ Strategy (czstrategy.com). CZ is a marketing strategy and inbound marketing firm in the Chicago area. He also founded RealityRN.com, a social site for nurses, which was sold in 2013.

3. Dave is a writer.
Dave was an editor (in a former life) and has written:

Death by Suburb: How to Keep the Suburbs from Killing Your Soul (Harper-One), and

Native Tongue: Translating Your Message into the Language of Prospects (Big Snowy Media).

4. Dave and his wife Jana are foster parents.
Jana dragged Dave to get licensed with the Department of Child and Family Services in Illinois in 2010. Dave now thinks that being a foster parent is one of the best decisions he and Jana have ever made! Their youngest child was adopted in 2014.

5. Dave was originally trained to be a pastor.
Dave took a right-hand turn not long after he earned his Master of Divinity degree and took a job as an editor. Then he returned to graduate school to work on his MBA right before starting CZ Strategy in 2000.

STEVE MATHEWSON

1. Steve has a wife, four kids, a dog, and lives in the Chicago area.
Steve and Pris' kids are all married, save one. And they have a full and expanding quiver of grandchildren.

2. Steve is a pastor.
Steve is currently pastoring CrossLife Evangelical Free Church in Libertyville, IL, a North Shore suburb of Chicago. He spent 20 years before that, pastoring churches in Montana.

3. Steve is a writer.
Steve has published several books, including:

Risen: 50 Reasons Why the Resurrection Changed Everything (Baker), and

The Art of Preaching Old Testament Narrative (Baker).

4. Steve is an adjunct professor.
At seminaries and colleges, Steve teaches undergraduate and graduate courses on preaching. His specialty is how to preach narrative literature from the Old Testament.

5. Steve is way too educated.
Steve has one doctorate and is working on a Ph.D. in linguistics.

6. Steve introduced Dave to fly fishing "back in the day."
Dave would like to claim superiority in all things fly fishing, but the original Master was Steve. But has the mentee now outrun the Master? Dave likes to think so.

7. Steve's wife Pris now says she wants to learn how to fly fish.
Could that be a problem? Dave is a bit worried.

About the "2 Guys and a River" Podcast

"2 Guys and a River" is our weekly podcast that seeks to help you catch more fish and to help you enjoy more the precious moments on the river.

We've caught a lot of trout in our time, but we are amateurs, not professionals. The guides at your local fly shop are the experts. And you are the expert. We're grateful for those who post their wit and wisdom on our Facebook page and web site.

Keep your comments coming!

There are several ways to make sure you receive every one of our fly fishing podcast episodes:

1. **Download a podcast app on your smartphone.**
The most common app used by our subscribers is "Podcasts."

After you download the app on your smart phone, then simply search for our podcast by typing in "2 Guys and a River" in the search box. You'll pull up our podcast. Yea!

Then simply click "subscribe," and you'll receive a notification on your app when a new episode appears. You can also go back and listen to past episodes.

2. Visit our podcast page on iTunes or Stitcher.
Then simply subscribe to the feed. We'd also love for you to rate our podcast on iTunes. It helps!

3. Be sure to subscribe to our weekly email alert.
We send out an email every Thursday with the week's article and podcast episode. You can subscribe by entering your email in the form in the right column on every page on our web site.

4. Listen to every episode.
We've published quite a few episodes, and we continue to publish one a week.

If you want to see a list of every episode we've ever published, visit our web site and click on the "Every Episode" link at the top of the page. You will be able to listen to every episode we've ever published.

5. Don't forget our articles.
We also publish a new blog post every week. To see every article we've published, visit our web site at 2guysandariver.com and click on "All Fly Fishing Articles."

What is better than
3,000 calories
at a local supper club
or chop house after
a day on the river?

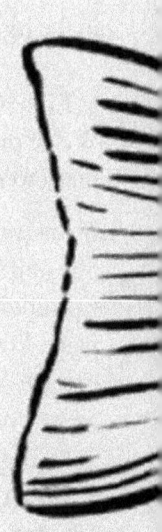

www.ingramcontent.com/pod-product-compliance
Lightning Source LLC
Chambersburg PA
CBHW060826050426
42453CB00008B/605